YOU HAVE TO STAND FOR SOMETHING,
OR YOU'LL FALL FOR ANYTHING

If you don't know what your position is, if you don't know where you draw the line between right and wrong, you'll never see yourself as you truly are. You'll never see the world as it truly is. You'll never have the confidence or the drive to do what you have to do to make a difference. You'll never feel good about yourself and your place in the world. So that's become my credo.

Stand for something.

And do you know what?

I don't fall for much.

As a young woman I was told (by some man, of course) that I shouldn't "rock the boat," that if I waited, good things would come to me. Yeah, right! I chose instead to listen to my mother, who told me that if I wasn't in the boat I should turn it over to make my point. That's the way I considered the law, that's how I now consider the media, and that's how I've approached this book.

Bantam Books

NEW YORK   TORONTO   LONDON

SYDNEY   AUCKLAND

You Have to Stand for Something, or You'll Fall for Anything

Star Jones

WRITTEN WITH DANIEL PAISNER

This edition contains the complete text
of the original hardcover edition.
NOT ONE WORD HAS BEEN OMITTED.

YOU HAVE TO STAND FOR SOMETHING,
OR YOU'LL FALL FOR ANYTHING

A Bantam Book

PUBLISHING HISTORY
Bantam hardcover edition published September 1998
Bantam paperback edition / November 1999

Grateful acknowledgment is made for permission to reprint from THE
PROPHET by Kahlil Gibran. Copyright 1923 by Kahlil Gibran and
renewed 1951 by Administrators CTA of Kahlil Gibran Estate and Mary
G. Gibran. Reprinted by permission of Alfred A. Knopf, Inc.

ISBN: 978-0-553-76213-6

Published simultaneously in the United States and Canada

Bantam Books are published by Bantam Books, a division of Random
House, Inc. Its trademark, consisting of the words "Bantam Books"
and the portrayal of a rooster, is Registered in U.S. Patent and Trademark Office and in other countries. Marca Registrada. Bantam Books,
1540 Broadway, New York, New York 10036.

PRINTED IN THE UNITED STATES OF AMERICA

For my mother,

who named me Starlet and taught me

to shine as brightly as possible

Contents

‿

I am the author
of the only dictionary that defines me.

—*Star Jones*

You Have to Stand
for Something, or You'll
Fall for Anything

Standing Tall

❦

The status quo sits on society like fat on cold chicken
soup, and it's quite content to be what it is. Unless
someone comes along to stir things up there
just won't be change.

—ABBIE HOFFMAN

SOMETIMES IT TAKES a story about death to
teach you about life. . . .

Back when I was working as a legal correspondent
for NBC News, I discovered what appeared to be an
appalling injustice in Esto, Florida, so I went down with
a production crew to check it out.

Esto is a sleepy little town on the panhandle, just
south of Dothan, Alabama, another small town. I remember thinking how cool it was to stand with one
foot in Florida and another in Alabama at this one place

in town, and that, in more ways than one, the region really was a kind of crossroads. I was there to look into the events surrounding the death of a local centenarian named Ada Dupree, whose passing split the town along racial lines in a way that seemed to beg for a spotlight.

Miss Ada—you'll forgive me, but I'm from the South, so every adult southern woman gets a "Miss" in front of her name—was one hundred and four years old at the time of her death, and one of the most beloved people in Esto. Along with her husband, she was one of the founders of the town, and over the years her good deeds and indomitable spirit came to characterize the community. People came from all over to visit with Miss Ada. She was even mentioned on *The Today Show* by Willard Scott, on the occasion of her 100th birthday, and she had a collection of good friends that would have filled the spaces between Esto and Dothan.

One of those good friends was Sybil Williams, the wife of the former local mayor. When Miss Sybil was a child, Miss Ada helped raise her, and in adulthood the two women were like sisters. Miss Sybil was in her late seventies at the time I went to meet her, which made her about twenty-five years younger than Miss Ada at the time of her passing, but I suppose at that age the difference in years didn't much matter. What did matter to these women was the bond of love and respect they'd built together, and the shared history of more than half a century.

Well, Miss Sybil was so touched by Miss Ada's passing that she made plans to have her buried in the Williams family plot at the Williams's church. It was where

Miss Ada wanted to be buried—with the people she loved, for eternity—and it was where Miss Ada's own family wanted her to be, as well. They knew the special connection Miss Ada felt for Miss Sybil and her family. The problem with this plan, it turned out, was that Miss Sybil was white, and Miss Ada was black. Some of the white folks in the church—the same white folks who loved Miss Ada when she was alive, who turned out to celebrate her 100th birthday, who counted themselves among her closest friends—did not want a black woman buried in their cemetery. Not even Miss Ada. It just wasn't the way things were done in Esto. The message, if you were black, was that it was okay to be the most loved person in the town; it was okay to be a doctor or a lawyer or even the mayor; but it wasn't okay to trespass on the final resting places of your white friends and neighbors. In the final analysis, you weren't worthy of the same treatment, the same respect. Well, when I got wind of what was happening I just had to go down and take the pulse of this community for myself. I mean, these were the 1990s. We stood at the gates to a new century. The reports we were hearing in New York were deeply upsetting in the way they suggested a dangerous kind of racism, more troubling than the racism born of ignorance or disassociation. Here you had a black woman who was not only accepted by her neighbors but embraced, and yet even these people couldn't get past the color of her skin.

Before I left for Esto, I called my grandma Pauline down in Badin, North Carolina, just to check on her and my granddaddy Clyde. I told Grandma about the story I was working on, and we talked about it. She was surprised at my surprise, because black folks and white folks weren't buried together in Badin either. I was shocked, and started to rant and rave about how we didn't have to take that kind of garbage anymore, but Grandma hushed me and told me to calm my little self down and think about it. Most people want to be buried with their "people," she explained. Not their particular *race* of people, but the people in their family. Now, *that* I could understand. But what about someone who wanted to be buried somewhere else? Surely we had come that far, but Grandma couldn't say because the subject had never come up in Badin, although if it did she guessed the folks there would react pretty much the way the folks down in Esto reacted to the news of Miss Ada.

Talk about your reality checks. Still, I needed some kind of rationale, so my first stop in Esto was a visit with Miss Sybil. She impressed me straight off as one phenomenal woman. She had me out in her yard, sipping lemonade, and I turned to her and asked, "Why are you taking this on?" Hers was not a popular position. The issue had had a real polarizing effect on the community. Some of the people had threatened Miss Sybil, as well as Miss Ada's family. "If you try to bring that nigger to our cemetery," they were told, "we're gonna have guns." Keep in mind, this was 1995, in the United States of America, and these good people with their hearts in the right places were being threatened by these others with their heads up their butts. It was enough to make you wonder who'd turned back the clocks.

By the time I'd breezed into town, the Dupree family had gone ahead and buried Miss Ada in the "colored" cemetery. This wasn't their fight, but it was Miss Sybil's, and she was holding on to her cause. She took a purposeful sip of lemonade and gave me the answer of a lifetime: "Baby girl," she said, "if you don't stand for something, you'll fall for anything. I would rather go to my grave knowing that I did what I was supposed to do, knowing I was on the side of right, knowing I stood up for a friend, than be complacent and simply go along with these people. If they don't like it, that's their problem."

I thought, Whoa! I don't think I had ever heard someone summarize exactly what I felt about life like this gracious woman did right then and there. Her answer shakes me up even now. I sat in awe, because in front of me I saw the woman I wanted to be. I wanted to be like Miss Sybil. I wanted to have the strength of character to stick to my principles, no matter what the argument was, no matter the stakes. It could be about race, religion, education, family, whatever. If you're on the side of right it doesn't matter who's coming at you. It doesn't matter if they're throwing stones. If you can go to sleep every night after having looked in the mirror—after having brushed your teeth and washed your face—and still find something to feel good about, to feel proud of, then you'll be fine when God finally asks the question, "Have you been My servant?" If you've been on the side of right, you've been His servant.

Miss Sybil had it exactly right. If you don't stand for something, you'll fall for anything. If you don't know what your own position is, if you don't know where you draw the line between right and wrong, you'll never see yourself as you truly are. You'll never see the world as it truly is. You'll never make a difference. You'll never have the confidence or the drive to do what you have to do, to do what you know is right. You'll never feel good about yourself and your place in the world. So that's become my credo. Stand for something. And do you know what? I don't fall for much. I know what I believe, and I know what I will do to support those beliefs, and everything else will just have to take care of itself. If it didn't matter to Miss Sybil what her friends and neighbors thought of her for taking such an unpopular position, then it doesn't matter to me what people think about some of the unpopular things that can't help but find their way out of my mouth. If I know it to be right and true, then that's all that matters.

In Esto, Miss Sybil's stand didn't amount to much beyond shining a light on the true nature of the folks who lived in that part of the panhandle. Miss Ada's body remained in the black cemetery, and Miss Sybil's fight couldn't change anything, but I realized it didn't matter. She didn't have to win the fight in order to be heard. She just had to stand.

Bringing Something to the Table (Other Than an Appetite)

❦

I don't know anything about luck. I've never banked on
it, and I'm afraid of people who do. Luck to me is
something else: hard work—and realizing what is
opportunity and what isn't.

—LUCILLE BALL

YOU WANT TO really piss me off? Come to me
with an insincere smile and tell me how wonderful it is
that "someone like me" is so articulate. Tell me how
"surprisingly well" I come across on television, or that
you're shocked sometimes to find yourself agreeing
with me.

It happens all the time—especially now that I'm on
the air every weekday on one of the big-three broadcast
networks—and I'm not always sure how to respond. I
try not to see things in black and white, but it's hard to

keep race from coloring this one. If it's a black person on the other side of the comment, I'm inclined to let it slide. A part of me can't help thinking, Well, you know, it's okay. I know my "folk" are sincerely proud of me and what I've accomplished, just as I keep a little bit of a rooting interest in the public (and worthwhile) successes of other blacks. But usually the comment comes from some other place, and it's laced with all kinds of backhanded nonsense. It's said with real astonishment that someone like me should have a clear thought in her head, a clear notion of how to communicate it, and a platform on which to do so. Underneath the comment is the unspoken assumption that I've come to the table expecting to be fed, without thinking to bring something to the party.

Come on, people. I'm a lawyer, for goodness' sake. I've gone to school, same as you. I've worked my butt off, same as you. I've thought things through. Do you really think, deep down, in those places we don't like to talk about, that I should be on the television, commenting on the latest development in a prominent trial, saying, "Dem people, dey done lost dey minds"? Is this the role you've consigned me to? Let me tell you, it's one of the most irritating side effects of my public life. Sure, I know that in their own way these people mean well. I know most people don't begrudge me my place at the table. But I also know we've got a long way to go before we truly judge each other as equals, without any preconceived notions of who we are and how we're supposed to be.

For years now, I've struggled with a way to respond to what I can't help but regard as a put-down. Let's face it, if it's not meant as an insult to me it still seems a veiled insult to my parents, or grandparents, or to black people in general. It's like telling someone she's doing okay, considering where she's from, considering the bad hand she's been dealt, but I don't see why we have to *consider* anything. There's no reason for any of us—black, white, yellow, *mauve*—to qualify our successes or justify our being here. None of us deserves to be judged by any lesser standard. We're all just doing the best we can with whatever package of raw materials we've been given, and we owe each other the simple kindness of leaving it at that.

I once mentioned this particular irritation to an older black woman in Buffalo, and she suggested that the next time some insincere, unenlightened, "well-meaning" bigoted person came up to me and told me how well-spoken I was, I should say it was because I was raised by white people. I laughed so hard I thought I'd need oxygen. Baby, it was the best comeback I'd ever heard, and I vowed to use it at first chance, but then when I thought about it some more I realized it wouldn't do. It may have been absolutely dead-on, but I started to think it was maybe a little bit too much for most people to get their hands around. And besides, with my luck the person would just look at me, open-mouthed, as if to say, "You were?" As if to say, "I knew it had to be something."

Yes, it's usually something, but in my case it's been hard work and strong family values and an abiding faith in God and justice and determination. These are the values I bring with me to the table, and along with them comes a deep appreciation for education. Very early on, even before junior high school, I imagined for myself a career as a lawyer, and it was always clear that school would take me there. For the life of me, I'm not entirely sure why I looked to the law, but I have some ideas, and most of them point back to my mother. She wasn't a lawyer, but she had gone to college and held a good job and set a fine example. One of her great lines was that you may have been born in the ghetto but the ghetto's not born in you, and she lived that truth. She taught me I could do anything, be anything, overcome anything. She taught me to honor the law and do what's right and stay true to what I know. She taught me to make myself heard and to speak my mind—respectfully, but loudly enough (and sharply enough!) to make my point. And she taught me well.

People tell me all the time how lucky I am, and I want to reach back and punch them in the nose. The kind of luck they're talking about has got nothing to do with who I am and what I've made of my life. My mother raised two little girls, for a while there on next to no income. She emphasized education above everything else. Go to school. Get good grades. Read. Do the right thing—for your community, for your family, but mostly for yourself.

If there *was* any luck in my equation it was the blessing of having Shirley for a mother. Shirley was always telling me I was worth it: worth the time, worth the trouble, worth the effort. Whatever it was, whatever was at stake, she always made sure I knew I was worth it, and that's a precious gift to give a child. My mother never told me, "That's not for you," or "You'll never achieve that." Not once. I don't even know what that would sound like, coming from my mother's mouth. I wasn't told anything but "You're the best." "You can do it." "It's all up to you." Shirley's expectation, always, was that I would kick ass, and make her proud, and the great thing was that she managed to make her expectations clear without putting any pressure on me. It was never "You *must* do," or "You *must* be." It was always "You *are.*" "Take it." "Go for it."

I suppose Shirley collected these same empowering messages from *her* mother—my grandmother, Pauline, a very unassuming, very wonderful lady who still wakes up some mornings and makes biscuits for her husband, my granddaddy Clyde. Grandma Pauline raised nine daughters in a three-bedroom house in North Carolina. (Actually, the third bedroom was added only after the ninth child was born, so for the most part it was my grandparents and eight girls in just two bedrooms.) I have a picture of the house and I look at it and think, What in the world? How did they fit eleven people in that house? By the grace of God, that's how, and with a firm and helping hand from my grandmother. She gave those girls a sense of family and a sense of belonging. They knew their place, and where they fit in the bigger picture, and that no matter what the world had in store for them they could always come home. And they had a father. Goodness, did they have a father! Clyde is a strong black man who worked hard, loved his family, and put God first. Out of that came a great sense of security. Out of that, my mother and her sisters could spread their wings and fly and know someone would always be there to catch them. They were free to dream, and underneath that freedom was the certainty that it was okay to fall short. They learned that what counts is going for it. Reaching. Trying.

Be clear, I'm not a believer in the notion that if you don't enter this world with the right parents you can't achieve anything. That's garbage. What makes the difference is the environment you're raised in, the support you're given, the opportunities you've seized and the ones you've made for yourself. A child born to extremely bright, wealthy parents can still be screwed up despite her station—or maybe even because of it. And a child born to uneducated, dirt-poor parents can still make as much of her life as she chooses. It's all in the foundation, and for me that foundation was knowledge through education. Knowledge is confidence and confidence is power, and in our house knowledge was key. Our Sunday outing was to the library, to see what new books came in that week, and the looming punishment for when I stepped out of line was to miss out. I'll tell you something: About the worst thing my mother could do was keep me from going to the library, because it was my favorite place to be. There were new worlds opened up to me on every trip. The first time I ever read about Paris, I went there in my head. More than that, I promised myself I'd go. Someday. And, indeed, when I finally made it to Paris I looked around and felt like I belonged, like my being there had been preordained, like I *knew*.

But our foundation wasn't just being book-smart. It was being able to open our minds to what was out there, to what was possible. It was, all around us, a supportive environment shot through with the message that what was out there was ours.

The first time I ever thought I'd be a lawyer I was watching *Another World*, with my other grandmother, Muriel. "Mama Muriel" (which we all pronounced "Merle") watched *Another World* every weekday I can remember, and I used to watch right along with her. (Now I'm completely committed to *All My Children* and my girl, Susan Lucci.) I was a little girl, maybe seven or eight, and I turned to Mama Muriel and said, "What's wrong with that lady? She's always in trouble." It didn't take a grown-up to notice this one character who couldn't keep herself from harm's way, from one week to the next.

Mama Muriel turned to me and said, "The child just needs a good lawyer."

"What's a lawyer?" I wondered.

"They're the ones who get people out of trouble," she explained. "You can rely on them."

"Well, then," I decided. "Guess I'll be a lawyer."

"You can be what you want to be, honey," my grandmother said. "Don't let anybody ever tell you different."

And that was that.

In our house, a declaration like this wasn't about to go unnoticed, and when it got back to my mother she was right with me. She didn't say, "Get out of here." She didn't say, "Aw, Starlet, let's be realistic." She didn't pat me on the head and tell me to get a trade, the way too many "well-meaning" teachers have told too many little black girls over the ages. Shirley would have put her foot up somebody's butt if they said that to me, but instead she just sat me down and helped me think it through. "All right," she said, "tell me, what's a lawyer?'' I told her what Mama Muriel had told me. Then she had me explain why I wanted to be one, and how I planned on getting there, and what we'd need to do, together, to see that it was possible. I had to get good grades in school, and I had to learn how to write well enough to apply for some of the scholarship programs they had in place to help us pay for all this, and I had to get started on it right away. ''If this is what you want, honey,'' my mother said, ''then I'm with you.'' And she was—all the way and from the very beginning. I was seven or eight years old and she had me planning, and keeping my eyes on the prize, and the funny thing is I never lost sight of that goal. I never went through those doctor-fireman-teacher-astronaut-ballerina-Indian chief phases. I always knew what I was gonna be, and I may have been the strangest kid on the planet, but I was blessed with the kind of mother who helped me not just to dream but to realize those dreams as well. So, yeah, I guess I was lucky, but not in the ways most folks tend to mean.

As a kid, I simply wanted to be a lawyer, but in high school I realized I wanted to be a trial attorney, and by the time I reached college I'd narrowed it down to prosecution. The assumption, when a young black woman looks toward a career as a trial attorney, is that she means to work for the defense, but as I mentioned at the top of this chapter, it's never a good idea to make assumptions about other people. I wasn't interested in defense. What I wanted was to be the gatekeeper. I wanted to stand at the edges of our criminal justice system and work to ensure that the right things happen to the right people, for the right reasons. I wanted to see that justice was served. At least, in theory, that's what a prosecutor is supposed to do, right? I chose prosecution because I wanted to do the right thing. Naturally, I have enormous respect for defense attorneys, and I'm the first to champion the good work they do, but for me the thrill lay on the side of the law, on the side of the people. I didn't choose to be a prosecutor for the money. (I made $22,500 when I came out of law school, which might have made a dent in all my student loans if I didn't have to eat, or buy a decent wardrobe for my courtroom appearances, or pay those ridiculous New York City rents.) I didn't choose to be a prosecutor out of any misguided power trip, and I certainly didn't have any designs on a political career. I chose to be a prosecutor because I felt it was what I was meant to do, and I meant to do it well.

In fact, I did it well enough that I was soon pulled by some of my more prominent successes in an entirely different direction. After six years in the district attorney's office in Brooklyn, New York, my officemate, Suzanne Mondo, wasn't the least little bit interested in what would turn out to be the opportunity of *my* lifetime. There was a new cable television network starting up called Court TV, and it was going to be the CNN of trials. At least that's how it was explained to me. They wanted Suzanne to offer running commentary during live coverage, but she passed the opportunity on to me. "Star," she said, "this is right up your alley. Why don't *you* do it?"

And so I did. I shot the pilot show with F. Lee Bailey (who I would come to know *quite* well in the coming years) and Harvard law professor Arthur Miller, and to tell you the truth I didn't once pull up and think to myself, Starlet, just who the hell do you think you are, passing yourself off among these prominent people? Going toe-to-toe with these giants in the legal field? Me? I'll tell you who I was—Shirley's daughter, that's who, and frankly, that's all the portfolio a person needs.

That was all it might have been, were it not for the way the nation sparked to Court TV's coverage of the William Kennedy Smith rape trial. My boss, District Attorney Charles "Joe" Hynes, thought it would be good publicity for the office to have a talking head with national television exposure, so he encouraged me to continue with my daily commentary as long as it didn't interfere with my job. The producers were happy to have me, and it seemed to be a good fit all around. And that's how this new career of mine started. In the beginning, though, I merely saw it as an extension of my role of being on the side of the people. I was a public servant in my full-time job, helping to put the bad guys away in a court of law; and I would be a public servant in my part-time but unpaid position, helping television viewers to understand a complicated trial.

Remember the William Kennedy Smith case? It was one of the first "celebrity" trials to play out under the intense public scrutiny we now take for granted, and it helped to inaugurate the gavel-to-gavel coverage of our most prominent trials on cable outlets such as Court TV and CNN and MSNBC. At the time, the American people couldn't get enough of the scandalous details that kept surfacing in the Kennedy case, and I was on hand to help Court TV viewers make sense of it all.

One of the big issues in the case, you'll recall, was over Patricia Bowman's inability to remember any of the details of the removal of her panty hose on the night of the alleged incident. She didn't remember whether *she* took them off, or whether *he* took them off, or whether she shed them on the beach or in the backseat of the car.

I happened to be appearing on Court TV the night after the panty hose flap surfaced in court, and as you can imagine, it was *the* hot topic on our program. F. Lee Bailey was once again joining me on the panel that evening, and he spent his time pontificating on Ms. Bowman's somewhat-less-than-total recall and how it might impact on her credibility in the eyes of the jury. His explanation was over everyone's head, and after a while the host turned to me and said, "Star, why is this an issue?"

"Well," I said, "it's been my experience that women know where they take off their underwear. When they don't, they have a credibility problem." I went on to explain that Ms. Bowman had been wearing control-top panty hose, and how no woman in the world could forget taking control-top panty hose off in the backseat of the car. (Trust me on this one.)

It was as if I'd split an atom with the pinky of my left hand. The reactions from critics and viewers and colleagues were overwhelming. I couldn't really understand it, at first. All I did was speak plainly, and tell it like it was, same as I'd always done, but I suppose television people weren't used to such fresh talk from their talking heads. James Blue, a booker at NBC's *Today Show,* was one of the people who took notice, and two days later I was sitting across from Katie Couric, offering commentary, and six weeks after that I had a contract to become NBC's legal correspondent.

Almost immediately, my role was recast; I was the expert, the voice of the people, the good girlfriend with the inside skinny. But I'll let you in on a little secret: I'm no expert. Me? Give me a break! I don't come to viewers as an expert, and I don't come to you as one here. I have tried fewer cases than a lot of other attorneys and practiced fewer years. I am not a scholar. I haven't written for a legal journal since law school. I am not a social scientist; I've never run control studies on the topics of the law or the media, and I don't plan to anytime soon. I am not a historian. I am neither a theologian who preaches nor an educator who teaches.

What I am, simply, is a lawyer and a journalist— schooled in the former and on-the-job trained in the latter. My job is to communicate. When I first started in television, I had some pretty starry-eyed notions of what it meant. Understand, I grew up watching television, and to be honest, I loved the bright lights and bigger paychecks and sudden recognition. But along with all these good things came a tremendous responsibility, and I've tried never to lose sight of that. I came to television with a set notion of what it means to the people who put their trust in the media in general and in television news personalities in particular. They deserve a media that's straight and fair and objective. They deserve to come ahead of some of the selfish goals that drive some of the media, on camera and off. Thankfully, I have had the benefit of working with some of the best the business has to offer. But, believe me, it's sometimes hard to look away from the self-serving nature of the television business and the people who work within it. The money can be great, and the perks fantastic, and there's nothing quite like the first rush of celebrity. But that's not what the media should be about, and I work to keep that in mind. I do this even though some of my colleagues and bosses I've had in television haven't expected me to be fair-minded and objective. Heck, most members of the media can't manage the same for themselves, so they're not about to be two-faced enough to expect any more (or less) from a rookie like me. Sometimes I even think that a lot of our viewers don't especially care if we're fair-minded and objective, as long as we're entertaining (and as long as we agree with them), but this doesn't change my obligations. As ever, it's my job to do what I take to be the right thing—even when most people don't see it the same way, most of the time.

Indeed, one of the first times I appeared on a talk show after joining NBC News, the host turned to me and asked if I was worried that some people would question my objectivity when I reported stories involving black people. I couldn't believe the question. I wanted to answer that I worried no more than white reporters do when they report stories involving white people, but I managed to bite my tongue. Instead, what I told the host was that I always chose to confront ignorance and racism with intelligence and excellence. I made Shirley proud with those words, but I still wanted to smack the host.

When I was a reporter, my job was to present all sides of a story. It wasn't to pass judgment, but to pass on the facts and give viewers the tools they need to make up their own minds. More than that, I realized early on that the viewers had a job to do as well, and that job is not to sit at home and absorb what we say just because we say it. Their job—*your* job—is to analyze, criticize, and keep us honest. Think. We may be watchdogs, and guardians of a distinctly American public trust, but *we* need to be watchdogged just as vigilantly as the good people working in any other distinctly American institution. That's bringing something to the table other than an appetite.

My world matters a great deal to me, just as your world presumably matters a great deal to you. I take my responsibilities as a television commentator and talk-show host as seriously as I took being an assistant district attorney. I'm determined to do the best job of it I can, and if these television people ever try to make me into something I'm not, I'm gone. I love my TV job but I don't *need* it. It doesn't define me, and it will never shake me from Shirley's firm foundation.

That said, let's consider the medium in which I now work. Television—network, syndicated, cable—is an incredibly powerful tool, and the images and messages we put out carry tremendous weight. It troubles me that our black children turn on the television and are unable to see other blacks in positions of power, or enjoying the same standards of living or quality of life as everyone else. And Hollywood executives wonder why African-Americans flocked in hit-making numbers to see movies like *Waiting to Exhale* and *Soul Food*. Despite lip service to the contrary, television executives are not especially committed to supporting quality black- and minority-driven programming, and from where I sit things don't look to be changing anytime soon. Can you believe that quality shows like *Under One Roof* and *The Gregory Hines Show* get canceled, while the step-and-fetch-it shows starring blacks, which celebrate buffoonery, keep getting renewed? And don't the people on *Friends* have any black friends? Even our advertising reflects a watered-down view. (How many black people do you know who go into a McDonald's and *sing* when they order a Big Mac? Thank God *those* commercials are finally changing.)

What can we do about it? Well, we must continue to bring something to the table—in this case, our indignation. We must demand better programming. We must write letters, make phone calls, and do whatever we can to insist that our television shows better reflect *all* of who we are—real people who care about our communities, our families, our schools. We may not have a *say* in what makes it onto our small screens, but we can register our opinion. We can turn the channel, or shut the set off, or take our spending dollars elsewhere. We can show our disapproval in every way available to us, and then we can go out and come up with a whole new bunch of ways no one's even thought of yet.

Look at it this way: You've all been invited to a fabulous dinner party. The places are set and the guests have been seated. Then the host turns to you and asks, "What have you brought to the table?" Will you stare blankly down at your empty plate, or will you have an answer? In many ways, this book is *my* answer. It's what I bring to the table—life lessons, learned truths, reasoned asides. It's what I stand for, and I've been working on it for the longest time. For as far back as I can remember, actually. As a young woman, I was told (by some man, of course) that I shouldn't "rock the boat," that if I waited, good things would come to me. Yeah, right. I chose instead to listen to my mother, who told me that if I wasn't in the boat I should turn the boat over to make my point. That's the way I considered the law, and that's how I now consider the media, and that's how I've approached this book you now hold in your hands. I'm clear on it. Don't expect me to "color" an issue because I'm black or female, but don't ever forget that I am. I bring my experiences, my biases and prejudices to the table, same as everyone else, and I'm entitled to them. But I also bring an understanding of other people's experiences, biases, and prejudices. Being black and female is not just a state of mind; it's a state of being, and I *be* every morning when I wake up and every night when I go to sleep. I recognize my responsibilities to my audience and to myself, but also to a community of people of color and women who take pride in my accomplishments.

And another thing: When racism and sexism don't apply, don't make them apply. It is not necessary to characterize every injustice as a racial thing or a gender thing, and doing so when they don't apply dilutes our legitimate concerns. It's up to all of us to shine a light on real cases of discrimination, and conversely to blow the whistle on anyone who seeks to use these issues as an excuse. Excuses are the tools of the incompetent, as we used to say in the Alpha Kappa Alpha sorority at American University; they build monuments to nothingness, and those who excel in them seldom excel in anything else.

All of which takes me back to the subtly racist comments that will forever come to me disguised as compliments: "Oh, my, you present yourself so beautifully." "You're so well spoken." Yada yada yada. To the people who choose to focus on how articulate I am, or how nicely I dress, or how comfortable I seem seated alongside an industry legend like Barbara Walters, let me say this: Get used to it. Start listening to *what* I say instead of *how* I say it. Let's accept these things as a given: Black people in positions of power or influence are going to be as articulate as white people in positions of power or influence. Successful women are going to carry themselves as proudly and confidently as successful men. It's how we get there, what we bring to the table. Sure, I understand that I owe my television career to the fact that a "window of opportunity" had been opened, and the concurrent fact that I was in the right place at the time of its opening. But this doesn't mean I was the only qualified black woman, or even the first qualified black woman, to step forward to fill the role. It just means that while I was standing there—qualified, capable, and determined—somebody opened that window and decided they needed a breath of fresh air.

And now it's up to me, and to all of you, to make sure there is a constant breeze. Rock the boat. Make yourself heard. Shake things up. And know that whenever you hear someone remark how well-spoken that Star Jones person is on television, you can always tell them she was raised by white people.

We Shall Overcome

❧

I have learned that success is to be measured not so
much by the position that one has reached in life as
by the obstacles which he has to overcome
while trying to succeed.
—BOOKER T. WASHINGTON

I HAD TWO kinds of growing up, and I wouldn't
trade one for the other—or either for a white picket
fence on a tree-lined street. Until I was six or seven,
we lived surrounded by fifty million aunts and uncles
and cousins in the small town of Badin, North Carolina.
(Okay, so maybe I exaggerate, but not by much.) Badin
was a good place to be, even when my mother was
away at school, trying to get a leg up.

Shirley was a young woman with a child born out of
wedlock—me!—and a determination to make her

mark. She was an independent spirit with a great support system in place to allow her to make some difficult choices. I don't agree with all of those choices, and I wouldn't have made the same ones for myself—but I'm sure glad she played her hand the way she did. Any other way and I wouldn't be here.

At twenty-one, she became pregnant by her college sweetheart, a man named Donald. They were at Winston-Salem College together, and they decided not to get married, but their families came from such a strong, southern, Christian place that they all agreed to help with raising me. At the time, about the only thing Donald had going for him was his tremendous family. He came up a bit short in my mother's estimation. She didn't want anything to do with him, long-term, and he didn't want anything to do with her. In all honesty, he really didn't want much to do with his child, judging by the role he played in my life or the amount of money he paid in child support or the effort he might have made just to stay in touch during those early years.

Under those circumstances, without the support of my baby's father, I wouldn't have had the baby. Shirley, however, was cut from a different cloth—and thank God for that. She had her own set of dreams, and I didn't fit neatly into any of them just then, but she made room for me in what ways she could. She went off to finish school at Rutgers University, in New Jersey, but only after she'd seen me lovingly situated with both sets of grandparents back in North Carolina.

For all his faults, Donald had a killer set of folks— my grandmother, "Mama Muriel," and my grand-daddy, "Daddy Paul," along with Donald's sister Shirley—filling some of the spaces my momma might have. And they loved me like crazy. They were good, big-hearted people, and for all practical purposes they shared custody with my grandma Pauline and my grand-daddy Clyde on my mother's side of the family. On top of that, Mom had about a half-dozen of her own sisters nearby, and there were all kinds of aunts and uncles looking after me, and—really—it was about the best kind of growing up a girl could have had. There were cousins, and family gatherings, and my mother wasn't gone much more than a couple weeks at a time. I was surrounded by love and comfort. Besides, this was the way of it for so many families in the South at that time. There was no such thing as an "illegitimate" child; all children are legitimate (it's the parents who are illegiti-mate), and back then, in North Carolina, we all had a place and a purpose in our families. It wasn't at all unusual for a single mother to leave her children with her parents or older siblings while she went off in search of an education or better opportunities than they could find back home, and it wasn't any kind of hard-ship. No, I wasn't with my momma every day, but I was with people who loved me, and I didn't want for anything. I never had the feeling I was missing out.

When my mother got her degree and a good job up North, we moved together to the Miller Homes hous-ing project in Trenton, New Jersey. Here again, it was a good place to be. I had good new friends all around. There were relatives—my uncle Jim and aunt Mary, and my uncle Eddie and aunt Doris. Mom worked for the city government, and she had a steady paycheck and the respect of our neighbors. I had a place to play. I even had a baby sister, Sheila.

So there we were, the three of us, carving out a new life up North, making the best of it. The contrast was stark, but mostly in a good way. Housing projects, when I grew up in Trenton, were mostly positive, working family environments. I don't know when that changed. Sociologically, I understand how and why, but I can't see the transition. I don't know when the projects became a place where drugs were bought and guns were exchanged and fifteen-year-old girls turned up pregnant. I don't know when children started not listening to their mothers. When I lived there, it was a good place to be, a safe place to be. You minded your momma and made the best of things. And you never wanted for another kid to play with.

The first trauma I knew as a child was secondhand, but Shirley brought it home. We were going on a class trip. We were in the fourth grade. We were allowed to go to the store across the street to buy chips and soda for the bus ride. Our moms had all given us money for the treat, and off we went—except one little boy, who didn't make it back across the street. The back story to the tragedy was we didn't have a traffic light on our corner. The parents had been complaining. It was a busy street, with the projects on one side and the stores on the other. The children were always running back and forth. It was, everyone always said, an accident waiting to happen—and sure enough, one finally did. I can remember turning around just as this little boy was hit by a truck. I can still hear the braking screech of the tires, and the bleat of the horn, and the sick thud of the collision. Try as I might, I can't call back the image of that little boy lying there in the street, but I obviously saw him. I was there. I must have blocked it out, or not taken it all the way in. I know there was a burst bottle of orange soda at his side, bubbling out onto the street, but I can't call back the look on the child's face, or what he was wearing, or how he had fallen, or whether or not there was blood. I can't remember the commotion all around.

Sometimes the mind helps you accommodate the unthinkable. I was eight years old and I wasn't ready to know about such things. (Who ever is?) Death wasn't a part of my world at that time in my life. I'd lost a great-uncle, but that was never set out for me as any kind of tragedy; he'd lived a full life; it was the way of the world. But here, with this little boy, the order was off. This wasn't the way of the world. I went to the funeral with my mother, in a small chapel they had set up at the Miller Homes. There was a viewing. They put the little boy in a white suit in a white casket with a little white Bible in his hands, and this time it registered. This time I took it all the way in. I'd had a couple days to talk it through with my mother. She told me what to expect, but what she couldn't tell me was how I'd feel. To see this little boy, about the same age as me, dressed in his Sunday best and as still as snow, was about the saddest, strangest experience of my young life. It wasn't real—because, of course, how could anything like the sudden death of a little boy be real? I mean, he didn't even get to finish his orange soda. It wasn't real, and yet it was more real than anything.

Out of this tragedy, though, came an enduring lesson. In the days that followed, Shirley was one of the neighborhood mothers who protested the traffic safety on our street. There was a sit-in right out there in the middle of Lincoln Avenue. It was a sign of the times—1970—and Shirley and the other moms all looked the part. My mother wore her big hoop earrings, and she had her head wrapped in a headdress, and she wore a dashiki. She looked like she'd just stepped off the set of *The Mod Squad.* I loved her for that look—and for the stand she made. I sat with her in the middle of the street, singing freedom songs, singing "We Shall Overcome," and I was overcome in a different sense. Really, I was overwhelmed by a feeling of real power, that a group of hardworking mothers and their children could divert traffic and make such a loud, peaceful mess and get people to notice. That we could make a difference.

Shirley even got arrested. My, I was so proud of my momma on that day. I was always proud of her, but on that day especially. We got that traffic light, and along with it a profound gift—the lesson that you could change things. The episode taught me, in real terms, that real power could flow from real people. No, you couldn't bring this little boy back, but you could change things. One day at a time, one step at a time, one person at a time. Even a group of lower-class working mothers could band together and make themselves heard and move mountains. It may have been too late to save this one child, but it was right on time for me.

I often wonder what might have happened to that little boy if the traffic light had been in place, or if the truck had been speeding down some other road, or if the split second of that moment had ticked more in the child's favor. I see his little face, all beatific and cleaned up in that white coffin, and imagine what his future held, and I don't come away with any certain fate. I can't picture him grown. All I know is that, as a young black man growing up in a housing project, the statistics say he'd either be in jail or dead. Hell, it's more likely he'd be in jail or dead than a college graduate. That's by the numbers. Of course, the numbers don't mean anything on an individual basis, and it's possible this kid could have developed a cure for cancer, or new ways to harness solar energy, but he didn't get to find out the rest of his story.

The rest of my story, though, had yet to be told, and I thank God every day that Shirley was willing to fight those numbers for her two girls. She didn't play it by the book, my mother, because if she had she would have never had me. I wouldn't have. I'm 100 percent pro-choice, and knowing what I wanted out of life at that age, knowing that I couldn't really depend on the man with whom I'd gotten involved, there's no way I could have reached my dreams with a baby in tow. And forget *my* dreams. There's no way I could have provided that child with what she needed. But if I became pregnant now I'd have the child. It's not what I want—to raise a child without its father, to settle down before this new career of mine has even started—but I have the financial and emotional resources to handle it, and therefore the obligation. And, not for nothin', I'm not getting any younger, so I would probably consider it a gift from God. But at twenty, no way was I ready to handle a baby.

As long as I'm on it, let me make my position clear: However she plays it, a woman has a right to make that choice, and I would fight to protect that right. We travel a treacherous path when we shed our rights and our freedoms, and this one cuts deep. I'm not suggesting that abortion is a good thing, but sometimes it's the best thing. Sometimes it's the only way out of a bad situation. I don't delude myself into thinking an unborn fetus doesn't represent human life. Oh, definitely, there's a life inside you; you're killing that life inside you, but it's not a life that can live on its own, and I can't see why our laws should take the decision to continue that pregnancy away from the woman. It's un-American. It goes against how I was raised and what I was taught, and yet at the same time I recognize that my beliefs aren't everyone's. If abortion is antithetical to your beliefs, then by all means don't have an abortion. But don't tell me what I can and cannot believe.

I may not have made the same choices as my mom, but I thank God for her choice of the man she would ultimately marry. When I was nine, she met a kind, sweet jewel of a man named James Byard—my stepfather, although I've never been comfortable qualifying the term. If anyone has earned the right to be my father, straight out, it's Jimmy, and that's how I think of him. He's my dad. My full-fledged dad. He's the one who showed me how a man is supposed to be. He's the one who held my head when I was sick, and my hand when I was scared. He's the one who taught me about boys. He's the one who understood the first time a relationship disappointed me. He's the one I hold out for.

When I graduated from law school, Donald gave me enough money to live in New York for the entire summer, until my job as an assistant district attorney began. I couldn't have made it without it, and it was very much appreciated, but it's still hard for me to pull a positive childhood memory of Donald and me—alone, together. I know we had them. I spent summers and school vacations with Donald and his family. I know that I get my taste for good North Carolina barbeque from him. I know we had a good time. But my most vivid memories are not of the two of us, alone, as father and daughter. They're of all of us together—Mama Muriel, Daddy Paul, Aunt Shirley, and Donald.

I do have a couple of painful memories. One Christmas, when I was fairly young, Donald kept promising he was going to get me a stereo. We couldn't afford a stereo, but Donald could, and he promised. He never paid any consistent child support (in contrast, his sister Shirley—bless her!—was extremely helpful, and I got through college and law school in great part because of her financial support), but he would send money and a nice gift once in a while. Anyway, Christmas Eve came and the stereo was not there, and my mother would not have me be disappointed. She went out in the middle of the night, with money we didn't really have to spend, and bought me that damn stereo. That's how she was, and she never let Donald forget that one slight. She never forgave him for it, either.

To this day, I still remember how I felt the time I went to North Carolina for one of my visits right after

Donald had gotten a very good promotion at work. He had long ago married a nice woman who I loved very much, and together they had two children. One of my favorite things to do during my visits was to look through Donald's old scrapbooks at the pictures of my mother when she was young. She looked like Dorothy Dandridge, all glamorous and done-up, and he had some great shots of her from their college days. He wasn't too bad-looking himself—a big, tall, handsome guy—but I was really looking for my mother. On this visit, I noticed that the local newspaper had published an article on Donald and all his professional accomplishments, keyed to his promotion. He had tucked the article into his scrapbook, and I happened upon it before too long. The article went into his educational background, and his social background, and his family background. At the end of the article, it said that he and his wife had two children.

I put that scrapbook down and wanted to cry. I don't think anything has ever hurt me as much as reading that line. It upsets me still. I didn't even occur to him. I couldn't say anything to Donald, because I couldn't let him know that it meant anything to me. I wanted to be strong about it. I told my mother about the article, though, and she tried to ease me past the pain, even though I knew deep down she wanted to kill him for hurting me yet again. She said, "Starlet, these newspaper people write what they want to write. They probably just took it off some bio." It wasn't like her to race to Donald's defense, but I loved her for trying this one time.

Years and years later, when I started in television, I

had to prepare my own press release, and I remember writing that my parents, James and Shirley Byard, lived in Trenton, New Jersey. I chose not to mention Donald at all, just as he had chosen not to mention me. It may have been petty and vindictive, but I didn't care. I told my momma what I'd written on the release before I sent it back to the public relations people.

"Make sure you're doing that for the right reasons," she said, "and not for the wrong one."

That's all she'd say, but I knew what she meant. She meant it was fine to honor Jimmy. He deserved it. But it wasn't fine to dishonor Donald simply because he'd hurt me the way he did. And she was right. I sent the release back as written, not because of the slight from Donald, but because of the place I had in my heart for Jimmy.

It's impossible to go back in time and set things right, and that's an important lesson for parents. You kinda reap what you sow, so be very certain, when you bring a child into this world, that you are emotionally, financially, physically, and spiritually ready to help form that young person's mind, body, and spirit. You have to be there. Because soon enough that child will be an adult, and you'll have to relate to her as an adult, and if you've made no impact you'll have a hard time maintaining any kind of relationship. When you realize, at fifty or sixty or seventy, that you are finally ready—emotionally, financially, physically, and spiritually—to reach out to that child, she'll be gone. Honey, she'll be long gone.

I'm not gone yet, as far as Donald is concerned. I've actually come to enjoy our occasional visits and chats.

Shirley, on the other hand, has very little use for him still, although she has mellowed from the long-held position that she would not cross the street to piss on him if he were on fire. It sounds harsh, I know, but my mother knows how to hold a grudge, and in this we're a lot alike. We're a lot alike in most things. We look alike. We've got an attitude alike. We see things the same way. We share negative traits as well. We're ornery alike. And stubborn. And we're not ones to forget. If you tick us off, or make us feel bad, or in any way do the wrong thing by either one of us, we will hold it against you for the remainder of our days. I can forgive, but I can't forget.

And things do come full circle. Recently, I received a note in the mail from Donald with an article describing the wonderful youth project he was involved in now that he's retired. It's a great program, and he should be proud of the work he's doing. Alongside the article, there was a little box in the corner highlighting some personal tidbits of information that usually accompany these things, and this time it listed "Starlet Jones" of New York as one of his children. (The reporter actually spelled my name wrong, but that's another thing.) After all this time, it gave me a certain level of satisfaction, but then I started to wonder if I'd have made the cut if I hadn't made a name for myself on television. Would I hear from him at all if I'd grown up to be a crackhead prostitute, or even an anonymous working stiff? Maybe. Maybe not. Maybe I'd just hear from him less often. Maybe I'm not being fair. Maybe there were other circumstances, other considerations at the time that I don't know about. Maybe something was said or done that kept him away. Maybe this was just the way it was supposed to be so I could grow up to be the woman I am.

I know that *not* having Donald's constant presence in my life helped to make me who I am, and for that, in some perverse way, I suppose I'm grateful. He taught me to rely on *me*. His absence helped to give me presence, and helped me to realize that I had to make up my own mind what I was going to achieve, and how, and that I had to go about achieving it on my own. I had the best mother on the planet, who later in life married a phenomenal man. She came from absolutely phenomenal parents; and Donald, for all his faults, came from phenomenal parents as well. Do you know how wonderful they were? When I was little, Mama Muriel kept a beautiful picture of my momma in her living room. I was living in their house at the time—kindergarten and first and third grades (I skipped second)—and as long as I could remember she had this picture out. It was one of those great college portrait shots, with the shoulder thing happening, and a little bit of cleavage, and maybe a little too much makeup. You've all seen that pose. Until the day she died, Muriel kept that picture out, long after Donald had met and married another woman. My grandmother's attitude was, This is my grandbaby's momma, so she's a part of this family. So that's the kind of people Donald came from. That's the kind of people I came from.

Unfortunately, a lot of young people out there don't have it so good. They don't have my momma's support mechanisms to help fill in the blanks. They have an absentee biological father, and in some cases an absen-

37

tee biological mother, and no extended family to take their places. There's no one. So what do you do in that circumstance? You look in. That's really what you do, and I know it's the hardest thing in the world. I know. But you find that place in your heart that allows you to be your own tower block. I love that phrase: tower block. I pulled it from a wonderful song by Julia Fordham. Gracious, that song impacted my life in a big way. It put me in the frame of mind where I knew that in order for me to achieve the things that I wanted to achieve, I would have to make Star the most important person in Star's life (God's guidance notwithstanding). I am, now and forever, my own tower block. In my life, it all flows from me and through me and because of me. And that's really what has to happen for children who grow up with crackhead mothers and absentee fathers and grandmothers who just can't handle another responsibility. They have to become their own tower blocks, because, honey, we shall overcome—we *can* overcome; we *must*. And we will. It's like my mother taught me on Lincoln Avenue all those years ago: Real power can flow from real people. It's just a matter of knowing how to tap into that power, and how to harness it and put it to work. If you can't rely on anyone else, then don't; rely on yourself. Even if you can rely on someone, like I've been able to do with my momma, and with Jimmy, and with my spectacular extended family, it still comes back to you. It starts with you and it ends with you.

There's a poem by Kahlil Gibran, from his brilliant book *The Prophet*, called "On Children," and it speaks directly to this theme. In fact, it was used as the lyric to a song by the wonderful folk group Sweet Honey in the Rock, and set to beautiful music. Part of it goes like this:

> *Your children are not your children.*
> *They are the sons and daughters of Life's longing for itself.*
> *They come through you, but not from you.*
> *And though they are with you, yet they belong not to you.*
> *You may give them your love but not your thoughts.*
> *For they have their own thoughts.*
> *You may house their bodies but not their souls,*
> *For their souls dwell in a place of tomorrow, which you cannot visit, not even in your dreams.*
> *You may strive to be like them, but seek not to make them like you.*

I turned out pretty okay, but there were a lot of people working on me. This whole package that you see on television every day? There were many hands in it. The smart, confident, funny, attractive woman on your screen could just as likely have been any of these young girls you see out on the street, but I had a bunch of help. I had a lot of support. I was given the basic tools I needed to overcome all the obstacles in my life, to get through the day, to succeed at whatever it is I've set out to do: self-esteem, confidence, dignity, purpose. A strong spiritual foundation. A sense of humor. A good heart. It's nice to have people all around to support you and comfort you, but these things are luxuries. Many people don't have these advantages, and they can still do okay. Absolutely, they can still do okay. They can still get that they can make a difference, and change things. They can overcome the worst of it and seize the best of it and make this planet a better place for us all.

That Sweet, Sweet Spirit

⌘

**I can do all things through Christ
who strengthens me.**
—PHILIPPIANS 4:13

THAT RIGHT THERE is my favorite scripture, and this right here is my favorite chapter. You readers should know that I'm smiling as I write this, because some of my fondest memories as a young person are rooted in church. It was the backdrop to my growing up. In one way or another, most of our happy moments as a family, and as a community, found their way back to whatever church we were attending at that particular time, and as I call those moments to mind now my heart sings.

My first memories go all the way back to Cedar Grove A.M.E. Zion Church, in Badin, North Carolina, which was where I spent the first part of my childhood. A.M.E. stood for African Methodist Episcopal, but we were essentially Methodists. Badin was a tiny little town, and as it turns out Cedar Grove was a tiny little church. When I was a child, it seemed to me about the biggest, grandest building I'd ever seen, but on my trips back as an adult I've realized the place was like a matchbook. To call it modest would have been overstating things a bit. I've been in studio apartments in New York City bigger than Cedar Grove, and yet it was all the building we needed. There used to be an outhouse in back of the church, although I couldn't say if it was ever used in my lifetime; there was plumbing as far back as I can remember, so perhaps the outhouse stood as some kind of reminder of the church's humble origins.

Its heyday was no less humble. I can still recall the smell—mildew, paint, old ladies' perfume—and walking into that teeny, tiny church, with its hard pews. Goodness, were those pews hard! My grandparents ran the church, and I always thought if I had a dime, I'd give my grandmother enough money to put some cushions on those pews. My granddaddy Clyde was the head trustee, and my grandma Pauline was the head trustee's aide. She put out all the communion wafers. She always wore a pretty white dress and a white hat and laid the doilies on the altar, and I used to sit down on those hard pews and marvel at my place in this wondrous little world. Baby, you've got to be important to touch the consecrated wafers, and if it was your grandparents doing the touching . . . well, that was something.

We had a little tiny choir (most of whom were members of my family), and I can remember singing some of those old Negro spirituals that just filled you up with a tremendous sense of family and purpose and hope. I still hear those songs in my head, and when one of them gets going real good I want to stand and sing. Sometimes we had a pianist, sometimes we didn't, but my memory doesn't need any accompaniment.

> *Blessed Assurance, Jesus is mine.*
>   *Oh, what a foretaste of glory divine.*
> *Heir of salvation, purchase of God.*
>   *Born in his spirit, washed in his blood.*
> *This is my story, this is my song,*
>   *praising my savior all the day long.*
> *This is my story, this is my song,*
>   *praising my savior all the day long.*

Almost everything about Cedar Grove was old-fashioned, even then. It was country. In certain respects, it was almost backwoods. But I loved that little church like I loved my own home. I loved the revivals, and vacation Bible school. The revivals were the social events of each season, and sometimes they could last the entire week, with a different preacher every night, or a guest choir. I loved the tacky little fans they used to hand out, sponsored by the local funeral home. On the front of the fan was a picture of a cute little boy and girl in prayer, and on the back was an ad for somebody's funeral home. That was our air-conditioning.

These days, they've put central air in that puppy, but the old ladies still fan. It wouldn't be a southern black church if the ladies didn't fan, and it wouldn't be Cedar Grove if Clyde and Pauline weren't running things, same as always. They're still there, my grandparents. They'll always be there.

For the other part of my growing up, church was also in North Carolina. Payne's Temple A.M.E. Zion. Those Methodists weren't much different from the Badin Methodists. Their hearts were all in the same place, and they were all just looking to make their lives a little richer through God's guidance. My Mama Muriel and my Daddy Paul were running things, like Pauline and Clyde, and they too were at the center of whatever was going on. Daddy Paul opened and closed that church every Sunday, and Mama Muriel had her favorite pew right near the front. She was a big woman, and she could belt out a song like there was no need for the invention of the microphone. Everybody would join in on her cue.

> *It's a highway to heaven,*
> *None can walk up there, but the pure at heart.*
> *It's a highway to heaven,*
> *I'm walking up the King's highway.*

Back home, church services never began with a minister calling people to prayer. They usually started with a devotional period, which incorporated this wonderful phenomenon of testifying. You'd stand up in front of your congregation, your family, your friends, your community, and tell the world what God had done for you. You'd testify. You'd lead the church in song. You'd offer a scripture. Something. You were always hearing these men and women testifying how the Lord had brought them from this misery or that one. "My husband left me, but I didn't need him 'cause God was there." Or "My children ain't doin' right, but as long as He is with me I can get through it." My grandmother's testimony was in leading the church in "It's a Highway to Heaven," and calling the service to order, and in doing so affirming her relationship with God in front of her community.

I think back to all those wonderful Sundays in both places, and I know that in their foundations I found the footing for my relationship with God. I talk about it on the air fairly often. A lot of times, you'll find people are uncomfortable speaking about religion in such a public way, and it usually makes television executives cringe (unless of course they're working for a religious station). I receive a lot of letters from people telling me how unusual it is to hear someone talk so openly about their Christian beliefs, and I suppose it is. Why is that? My television colleagues will encourage me to talk about sexual topics on the air. They'll encourage me to talk about race. They'll encourage me to talk about violence, or politics, or abortion. But the single most important aspect of my life, my relationship with God, should be off-limits? I don't think so.

We each find God in our own way. Or we don't look for Him at all. It's a private, personal journey that some of us choose not to make, but even that choice is private and personal. I don't pass judgment on people for the choices they make, and I won't abide others passing judgment on the choices I've made for myself, but once God has been revealed to me in this way, it would be violating my faith not to follow His rules. I've got to talk about it, on television especially. It's my way of testifying to my community. (Now that I'm on national television five days a week, I just happen to have a megacommunity!) The thing is, if you listen carefully you'll hear that my testimony is not about a religion. It's about my relationship with God. That's what matters to me. Everything else is gift-wrapping. It's how you dress it up and make it look all fine and pretty. But it's what's inside that counts.

I don't mean to get on a soapbox and suggest that I do everything I'm supposed to do. No way. I don't always walk as Christ would have me walk, but I try. I don't always think as Christ would have me think, but I try. I don't always live by the Good Book, but at least I know what pages I'm skipping. I know that I've been blessed with a certain amount of success, and with that blessing comes an obligation to give thanks to God, and to pass some of that success around. I can be funny and frivolous about wanting to go to Paris or to some hot new restaurant, but I know that I am as successful as I am because of the blessings of God. I know this. I know it like I know my own name.

In those letters I mentioned, people are constantly writing to ask how I can be so sure God exists, and I have a ready answer: I walk. I breathe. I laugh. My laugh is distinct from yours. When I smile my eyes light up in a way that no one else's eyes light up. Man can't make these distinctions. I know how it makes me feel to step on an airplane and say my little prayer. "God, guide this flight on the wings of Your angels and get us there safely.'' I say these words and I go to sleep, certain I am in God's hands. I feel it so strongly. I try not to focus on death, because it makes me anxious and nervous, but I'm not afraid to die. I don't want to die, but that's more out of selfishness than any fear of the unknown. I don't want to miss out on anything. Some good gossip will be going on down here and I don't want to miss a beat. That's where my anxiety comes from. But there's no uncertainty about the rest of it. There's never a doubt about what's waiting for me, and if something should happen to my plane, or if some other accident or illness should claim me before my time, I know I'll be in His hands. I know where I'm gonna be. I know my Mama Muriel's there, belting out her hymns. My Daddy Paul, he's there too. All my relatives and friends, people I haven't seen in ages, they'll be waiting on me. My friend Mark Grice, who took me to the prom and died of AIDS. He's there, and I can tell him what he meant to me. And when I get there, I can say to my grandmother, ''Nobody makes white potatoes like you did,'' because the truth is I have not had a good white potato since she's been gone and I'd like for her to know that.

Now that I'm on it, that woman could sure cook, and most of her cooking and fussing in the kitchen had in one way or another to do with the church. She was always cooking for our guest ministers, and organizing the spreads for our church socials and revivals, and trying out some new recipe on us before preparing a plate of the same for the next event. For some reason, in North Carolina, church always seemed to be about food. It was about what so-and-so was bringing. Did you make a cake, or were you signed up for potato salad? Or maybe it was the fried chicken? My cousins and I had our favorite people who'd cook for us. We'd be off in the corner, trying to figure out who made the chicken and whether or not it was worth eating. If it was "Miss Anne's," we were okay, but we knew whose chicken not to eat. Some of these women just could not cook. I'm sorry, but they should have signed up to bring the paper plates or the plastic silverware, because their food had no business being put past other people's lips, but nobody had the heart to tell 'em. We kids knew, though. We knew who made the best macaroni and cheese. We knew whose fruit salad was usually left to soak in liquor overnight. We knew Miss Henrietta made some killer apple turnovers. Believe me, you've never had turnovers like Miss Henrietta's. That woman made the best dessert any human being ever made. As much as I love those flaming peaches at La Tour d'Argent in Paris, they can't touch Miss Henrietta's apple turnovers. Plain dough. Butter on top. Apples that she had cured with some cinnamon. She'd shove 'em in the dough, and press, press, press on the ends, and deep-fry those babies in the pan. Honey, that's some eatin', right there.

The church was my community as a child. It was my social center as much as it was my spiritual center. I was too young, really, to understand a lot of what was going on, and so what I took in had mostly to do with how secure I felt, how comfortable I was among all those good people. It wasn't until I was a bit older, after we'd moved to Trenton, New Jersey, that I started to look on church as the place to develop and refine my relationship with God. If you want to separate my life, I guess you could say that in childhood I was entertained by religion, and comforted by the familiar social aspects of it, and during my teenage years I finally thought to figure out what was going on. I wanted to learn all I could.

I attended parochial school at Notre Dame High School in nearby Lawrenceville, New Jersey, and part of our curriculum was a class on religion. For the first time, I started to really understand what Catholicism was all about, and they couldn't teach me quick enough. The more I learned, the more I needed to know, and for a while there I started thinking seriously of converting. I started thinking maybe Catholicism was where I was meant to be, but then the more I learned the more I realized it wasn't where I was meant to be at all. It was interesting, my brief fascination with the rituals of it, but it was fascinating mostly as an exercise, and mostly for the way it got me to clarify some of my own opinions about religion. Please don't get me wrong, but the trappings of Catholicism started to bother me; but more than that, I became troubled by the role of the priest as a kind of go-between. I didn't believe you have to go through anybody to get to God. I won't ever believe that. Why should I have to go to a priest to tell the priest that I screwed up? So that he could go to God on my behalf? What, the priest has access to His private line? It made no sense to me. There's no need for any middleman. Christ already took that on, so I can't see the need for a mortal to help me get to God. My knees bend the same way as anyone else's. Remember, this is *my* relationship with God.

In Trenton, we belonged to Shiloh Baptist Church, which was led by the Reverend S. Howard Woodson. My parents are still members, and at the time it was probably the most elegant church in town. It was a stylish, happening place, about a century removed from Cedar Grove, but there was some good preaching going on there, and the Reverend Woodson offered a strong counterweight to some of the issues I was grappling with on my own. He and Deacon Ollie Green, who I still think of as my godfather because he baptized me, were tremendously helpful as I was sorting through these uncertainties. They answered my questions. They asked me to consider theirs. And underneath they provided another fine backdrop to my personal odyssey. The church wasn't just a place to go to be entertained, although it was surely that. It wasn't just a place to go and sit with my girlfriends and chew gum in the back of our Sunday school class, although it was surely that as well. No, it was actually a place to tend and nurture a transformation in me that had as much to do with intellectual curiosity as it did with spiritual devotion.

In college, at American University, one of the first things I did was join the gospel choir on campus. We had one of the best gospel choirs in all of Washington, D.C., and we traveled all over the region to perform at churches and neighboring universities. We could sing the roof off of any building, I don't care how big it was. Here again, I was in the midst of another transformation, and this time it was the music seeing me through. I listened to the words of the gospel songs and they started to move me in ways I had never been moved before. Realize, I'd heard all these songs my whole life —they were as much a part of me as Miss Henrietta's apple turnovers—but I never really listened to them until I joined the choir. "Call Him Up and Tell Him What You Want," or "I'm Looking for a Miracle." Those were some of my favorites, and the spirit behind them was, if there was anything you wanted in life, all you had to do was ask, and reach.

Singing those songs, I started to feel I could go to God with anything. I could give Him a wish list for what I wanted out of life, and I trusted that if I did my part, God would do His.

While at college, I attended the Mt. Sinai Church in northwest Washington, but it was my time in the choir that defined this period for me. I loved to sing, but I especially loved to sing gospel. I loved to sing His praises. It filled me with a sense of purpose, and pride, and well-being. It gave me faith, and during my senior year, when that faith was tested, God came through with flying colors. He passed that test not because *I* emerged at the other end of my ordeal alive and healthy, but because I had been able to depend on that faith. I felt secure in it, and I came away knowing that this relationship I shared with God was not manufactured. I wasn't deluding myself into believing something that wasn't real. It was absolutely real—so real I could rely on it during times of tremendous uncertainty and fear, and in times of great happiness. It was a part of me.

My major religious transformation came about during law school. I was entertained and comforted as a child. I was seeking a little something more as a teen-ager. I was starting to find some of the answers I was looking for as an undergraduate. But my relationship with God truly took hold once I joined the Windsor Village United Methodist Church in Houston, under the spirited guidance of the Reverend KirbyJohn Cald-well. We've since become friends, but I'll never forget how we came to know one another. I first heard KirbyJohn preach at another church in town, St. Mary's, where he was a young associate pastor, and I was awed. For the first time in my life, I recognized that there was a difference between a preacher who simply preaches and one who can preach and teach. KirbyJohn fell right at the top of the latter category, and the message of his sermon that day was to never allow anyone to place a "period" in your life. Other people can put down commas, or dashes, or semico-lons, he said, but only God can end the sentence. I liked that. I liked that no one is equipped to tell you a thing is over, and I thought, Yeah, this is how it's supposed to be. Each of us, in our relationship with God, must decide how far we can go.

Well, I'll tell you, KirbyJohn just blew me away. He truly did, not least because he was from the same generation as me. I was used to listening to these long-in-the-tooth preachers, who stood as much as authority figures as spiritual leaders. No matter how good they were—and they all had their strengths—the preachers in my life had seemed to be walking over familiar terri-tory. Every sermon was a little bit like the one before, and the one that would follow. It had gotten to where I could almost anticipate what they would say next, once

I knew their theme. But here was this young guy, no more than ten years older than I was, talking about some of the very issues I was weighing for myself. And he wasn't just talking about them. He was placing them in a religious context, and coming at them from some surprising angles, and motivating those of us in church to take control of our lives. I felt KirbyJohn was preaching directly to me, and when I found out he was taking over at Windsor Village I just had to follow him.

Now, Windsor Village wasn't the easiest church in Houston for me to attend. It was still inside the city limits, but about as far removed from the University of Houston's law school campus as you could get. It took some time getting there, but it was absolutely worth the effort. And I wasn't the only one making the trip. There were less than one hundred people at the church when I first joined, and in fifteen years the congregation has grown to over ten thousand members, so that should give some idea how rare it was to find a preacher with KirbyJohn Caldwell's gifts. Rarer still was the preacher who could live up to such a powerful first impression, but every service in Windsor Village seemed brand-new and exciting and wonderful. For my money, KirbyJohn Caldwell is the most brilliant preacher of the gospel you could ever hope to hear— truly, he wins going away—and yet he'll be the first to tell you of his limitations. He can only preach the words, he'll say, but it's up to each one of us to make them come to life for ourselves, and that's the profound lesson I took away from my time under KirbyJohn's guidance.

I've yet to find another preacher to match his brilliance, but I've discovered that every preacher has something to offer if you bring something to the service. It's like the title I slapped on one of the first chapters of this book—"Bringing Something to the Table (Other Than an Appetite)." Well, you've got to bring something to the pew other than your body. It's not enough to just haul your behind into church every Sunday and expect to have your spirits lifted for you. You've got to help with the lifting. You've got to bring your mind, and your soul, and a willingness to look at the world in a new way. And, most of all, you've got to bring your relationship with God, because without it, we're nothing. There's no preacher who can bring you closer to God if you're not able to take the first step yourself.

As an adult, in every place I've ever lived—Washington, Houston, Brooklyn, Los Angeles—one of the first things I've done is join a local church, and I haven't always looked for the same things. I'm not as concerned with the doctrine or the denomination as I am with the lessons I can learn from the minister and the congregation. My background is mostly Methodist, but it doesn't much matter. Methodists, near as I can tell, are very much grounded in tradition. There are certain songs that are always sung, certain prayers that are always read. The order of the service is essentially set in stone. Baptists are a lot more fluid, depending on where you are. You could have a service that lasts for thirty minutes, or a service that lasts for four hours. The Church of God in Christ is an interesting blend of southern Baptist and southern Methodist traditions, so I felt at home at the West Angeles Church of God in Christ when I was out in L.A.

Pentecostal churches have a much more hands-on feeling to them than you'll find in the other churches I've described. That's where you'll hear people speaking in tongues, where people are free to shout out in church, where the Holy Spirit can enter a person's body and you can actually see it. Now, I've got nothing against anybody's beliefs, and if you've found a way to God that works for you, I say you should just go for it and stick with it and pay no attention to a blowhard like me. But I find all that activity distracting. One of my good girlfriends tells me she can't go to a church that will cause her to miss her blessing, and I feel the same way. I'm there to be blessed in the house of God, and if there are all these people running up and down the aisles screaming and shouting I might just miss my blessing. For me, I like to go to a church where there's good singing, good preaching, and preaching that teaches. I'll leave all the bells and whistles to other folks, and take the basics for myself.

In New York, I've started attending the Central Baptist Church in Manhattan, because it offers a nice mix of what I found at Shiloh in Trenton and Windsor Village in Houston. In my heart, though, there will never be another place like Windsor Village because there will never be another minister like KirbyJohn Caldwell. KirbyJohn and I are friends to this day, and I'm sure to thank him every chance I get for teaching me once again that church should be a place for fun and uplifting and entertainment. He's brought me full circle, back to the comfortable community elements I cherished from my childhood churches in North Carolina. Every New Year's Eve, he put on a program called the Jam for Jesus, and he had that place jumping. When I lived in Houston, KirbyJohn would have all the great choirs in the city come down, and we'd get our party on, and the church was packed. You couldn't get in. Seriously, if you didn't get there early enough, you couldn't get a seat, and that's the kind of juice and excitement he was able to pump into that place. It was an exciting new spin on those old-fashioned revivals we used to have back home, and when we spilled out into the new year we were as revived as a person had any right to be.

And so I sit here now, with a silly old smile on my face, reflecting on the churchgoing experiences of a lifetime, and I realize that it's all of these experiences, taken together, that have formed my relationship with God. Right now, that relationship is about knowing. There was a time when it was about comfort and familiarity. There was a time when it was about asking questions. There was a time when it was about understanding the answers to those questions. There was a time when it was about discovering new ways for my spirit to soar. And now it's gotten to where all these things are a part of me. They are who I am. That's my testimony.

Awakening

❦

Destiny is not a matter of chance; it is a matter
of choice. It is not a thing to be waited for;
it's a thing to be achieved.

—WILLIAM JENNINGS BRYAN

I WAS EATING Chinese food when I first noticed
it. I was twenty years old. There was a strange feeling
in my chest. I thought it was indigestion, maybe heart-
burn. I didn't think it was any kind of big deal, and me
being the doofus that I am, I ordered a Pepsi, thinking,
you know, probably all I needed was to burp and this
strange feeling would go away. That's all it was, at first,
a strange feeling.

I called my mom when I got home. I was away at
school, at American University in Washington, D.C.,

majoring in the Administration of Justice, and I was in the habit of calling my mother whenever things didn't appear right. It was the August before my senior year, and I was living off campus, in Chevy Chase, Maryland. I was fairly self-reliant—earning good money as a part-time word processor, looking ahead to my senior year and my first semester as national vice president of my sorority—but I wanted to hear my mother's voice. In her voice was comfort, reassurance, company . . . whatever I thought I needed at the time. I was a young woman, but I was still a little girl.

"I'm not feeling well," I said to my mother on the phone. She was up in Trenton, New Jersey.

"Did you see a doctor?" she asked.

"It's not bad enough that I need a doctor," I said. "I think I just need to burp. It's probably just gas or something." I told her I wasn't in any kind of serious pain; I was just uncomfortable, and maybe a little worried.

"Starlet," she said, "you need to learn to go to the doctor when you're not feeling well." She went into a whole thing on health insurance, on how if you've got it you might as well use it, and I only half listened. "There's a doctor on campus," she tried. "Why don't you go see him?"

"I could go to the infirmary," I said, "but I really don't think I need a doctor. Maybe I should just lie down and go to sleep."

So that's what I did. Tried to, anyway. I tossed and turned all night long, but I must have nodded off, because I woke up the next morning and I was unable to move. I couldn't lift my arm to put my clothes on, and when I tried I got a searing pain in my chest. It was like nothing I'd ever felt before. I knew immediately something was wrong. Big-time wrong. I started to cry —not because I was imagining the worst (I tried never to imagine the worst), but because it just hurt so much to move. It hurt to breathe.

My roommate Ladonna was out of town, and I didn't want to worry my mother just yet, now that whatever was wrong was something more than indigestion. I hushed the little girl in me and played it like a grown-up. I'd call my mother when I knew a little bit better what was going on, and instead called one of my sorority sisters. It was all I could do to reach the phone and dial. I told my ''soror'' (that's what we call each other in Alpha Kappa Alpha) what I was feeling, and she said to call 911. She said she'd meet me at the hospital.

I don't know how long it took for the ambulance to arrive, or how long it took for her to meet up with me at the hospital in Bethesda, but it felt like forever. Probably it was fifteen or twenty minutes. Not long. But I was alone, and starting to feel afraid, and in so much pain; really, it was starting to hurt like crazy. Finally, we pulled up to the hospital and they wheeled me in on a gurney, and the doctors started working on me like I was having a heart attack. This is what happens when the patient complains of chest pains. They hooked me up to all kinds of machines; they did the EKG; they ran tests. And nothing was showing up. There was nothing irregular with my heart, and yet they could see I was in great pain. Then an intern noticed a tiny black blip on one of my X rays. He brought it over to show me. "I really can't tell you what it is," he said. "I've never seen one of these before."

I thought, Oh, great. Just what I needed, to be making medical history.

They did some more tests, took some more pictures. And I waited, alone on a stretcher in a hospital hallway. I lay there wondering what these people would tell me, when they'd get around to it, what I'd tell my mother.

You know, it's funny, but when you're lying around like that, in a hospital hallway, your mind starts bouncing from one scenario to the next. I tend to be an optimistic person, always looking for the silver lining, but just then, with all the time in the world to consider the fact that my time,might just be running out, I went a little crazy. Quietly crazy. I didn't kick or scream or break into a cold sweat, but I started to think things through. I wanted to consider everything; if it was fear, it was a pragmatic kind of fear; I needed to try on every possibility.

A voice pulled me from my suspicions: "You're probably gonna want to call somebody." It was one of the doctors. So much for full disclosure.

"My friend's on her way," I said. "Don't make me wait for her. Tell me now."

"We're gonna need to admit you," he said. "We need to see about that mass in your chest cavity."

I loved the way he used the word *mass* to protect me from what it really was: a tumor. Most likely a big one, from the grave look on his face and the practiced tone in his voice.

I called my parents and told them they needed to

come to Maryland to meet me at the hospital. I told them what little I knew, which turned out to be just enough to freak them out on the few hours' drive from Trenton to Bethesda. In the meantime, the doctors needed to drain my lungs. Apparently, the pains in my chest had to do with fluid in my lungs, which in turn probably had to do with a cold I wasn't taking care of. The tumor was something else.

By the time my parents arrived, the doctors were planning to take me in to do a biopsy, but my mother prevailed on them to let me have the procedure done back in Trenton. My parents were city workers, which meant their insurance was back in Trenton, but more than that they wanted me close to home. I'd have to be in the hospital a week, and they wouldn't have to take off so much work to be with me if I was local. It was a practical request, and the doctors agreed, as long as I was taken immediately from Bethesda to a hospital in Trenton. They bundled me up and put me in the back of my parents' car and we headed back to Trenton.

Man, I was pissed. The last place I wanted to be was in Trenton. My life was in Washington. I had things to do. School was starting the next week. I needed to get going on my law school applications. There were parties. I couldn't understand why I couldn't have the stupid biopsy done there, in the hospital in Bethesda. No way in the world was I thinking this was something serious. It was just something to be gotten out of the way. Yeah, it was a tumor, a mass, but I was thinking, you know, Do the biopsy and get me back to school before it starts. This was August, and school was just around the bend, and on top of that I had all these word-processing jobs lined up. See, I could type about ninety words per minute, and everyone else I knew had their little work-study jobs at $3.50 an hour, and I was pulling down $8 or $9 an hour, so I was doing okay, and I'd been hoping to bank as much money as I could before the semester started. So I wasn't thinking about any tumor.

I slept most of the drive back home. The doctors had given me some medication to keep me comfortable, and it just knocked me out, and I lay there, all balled up in the backseat of my father's old Mercedes, completely unaware of the drama unfolding in the front. I have no idea what my parents talked about on that long drive to the hospital in Trenton, but they must have been out of their minds. I learned later they were keeping things from me. They knew what was going on. They knew this was serious. My mother was so tense she nearly lost it when we arrived at the hospital. My room wasn't ready, and she started to steam. She said, "My baby is in pain, lying in the car, and you will find her a room!" My father just paced, back and forth, but my mother was on the prowl. It was like that scene in *Terms of Endearment,* where Shirley MacLaine tells the doctors to give her daughter something for the pain, except that the movie's Shirley didn't have a damn thing on *my* Shirley. My mother felt this was something that should have been taken care of. We had enough to worry about without worrying about a room.

They scheduled the biopsy for the next morning. They were going to open me up and take a piece of me out and send it to Pathology. I still wasn't freaking out the way my mother was freaking out, because at this point nobody had said the words *cancer* or *inoperable* in my presence. They all knew things they weren't telling me, but I was fixed on the procedural aspects. That's all it was, a procedure. I'd had my tonsils out when I was a kid, and I was thinking this would be the same. They'd get in, take what they had to take, and that would be it.

Well, that wasn't it. They did the biopsy, and I ended up staying in the hospital for seven days—and with a small scar at the base of my neck. It took a while for the results to come back, and I was weak from the surgery, and by the time they cleared me to go home they still didn't know what the deal was with this mass. The first indication my situation was going a little bit beyond routine was that we had to go back to the hospital to hear what the doctors had to say. I thought, This can't be good. When they want you to come in to get the results, it's not a good sign.

And it wasn't. It turned out that the tissue they'd removed was benign; there was no cancer, but because of the location of the tumor, it was inoperable. It was a tumor of the thymus gland. It's called a thymoma—one of the rarest tumors you can have. In most people, the thymus gland shrinks and goes away after puberty. You don't need it anymore. I didn't need it either, but mine didn't go away, and it developed a tumor and it kinda grew behind the thyroid and wrapped itself around the esophagus, between my lungs and my heart. The doctors explained that any one portion of that mass could be cancerous, but they couldn't get to it because of where it was, and even if it wasn't cancerous it would keep growing to where it would basically choke the life out of me.

My first thought, you know, was that this was something they could have told me straightaway. They didn't need a week to figure this out. It showed up on the X ray, and they could see it when they cut me open, and yet they still kept us stewing for seven days. I figured they were just waiting on Pathology to tell them it was malignant, and then they wouldn't have to go into all this other stuff. They'd just tell me I had cancer and that would be the end of it. But I didn't have cancer, not that they could tell; what I had was a genuine science-fiction movie growing in my chest, and people in white lab coats were telling me I was in trouble.

My parents had a tough time with the doctor's explanation. "So, like, what does this mean?" my mother kept saying. "What does this mean?"

My father kept patting her hand, sandwiched between his.

I'm the one who finally asked the question. "Does this mean I'm gonna die?" I asked.

"Don't be ridiculous," my mother shot back, but the doctor didn't flinch. That's when I knew it was bad. Right then, I knew.

"It's not a good prognosis," the doctor said.

"What does that mean?" I asked. My mother'd gone silent; Daddy kept patting her hand.

"The tumor is growing," the doctor said, "and it's inoperable."

"How long?" I asked all the tough questions. (I always do.) I was the lawyer, even then. I wasn't crying. My mother was crying. I'll never forget her tears, but I wasn't crying. I wouldn't let myself cry. "How long?"

"Nine months to a year."

At that point, my body did a little shudder. It was like my mind was ready for anything, but my body couldn't take the news. My mother started asking all the questions, and I just zoned out and was silent. I could hear them talking, but I was only half listening. Something about how radiation might prolong my life because it would shrink the tumor, but at the same time how my body couldn't take the constant radiation, so what was the point? Even with just half an ear, I had heard more than I cared to. "I'm going back to school," I announced plainly.

It was as if I'd said I was having a sex-change operation. "This is not the time to discuss this," my mother all but shouted. She wasn't hearing it.

"It's exactly the time to discuss it," I said. "I want to go back to school." Then I turned to the doctor. "Is there any reason I can't do this radiation in Washington?" I asked.

My mother didn't give him time to answer. She was frantic. "It's not the time, Starlet," she insisted.

Even Daddy tried to shut me up. "You heard your mother," he said. "We can talk about this later."

I'm the one who was just told she had nine months to live, and no one thought I had anything worthwhile to contribute to the conversation. It wasn't about me, I was quickly understanding, it was about *It,* this thing that was growing inside of me. It had already taken over, and I'd only just found out about it.

I allowed myself to be talked down from my position, or at least to be distracted from it for the time being, and we drove home in eerie silence. There was nothing to say. I sat in the back—furious at having to miss school, furious at having been talked out of what I wanted, furious at this . . . thing—and listened to my mother's sobs and tried to figure what they meant. Then she said something that knocked the wind right out of me. "I've got to tell Donald," she said.

Remember, my mother thought my biological father couldn't pour piss from a boot with the instructions on the heel, so the fact that she wanted to share this latest news with him was troubling. That was the first time it really registered. I thought, If she's willing to even talk to Donald it must be serious. My body did another one of those little shudders, and I deepened my resolve to play out the next nine months in my own way.

"I'm going back to school," I mumbled, mostly to myself but loud enough that they could hear me up in the front seat.

We got back to our house—a second- and third-floor walk-up on Edgewood Avenue. I remember that we received a phone call from the doctors within an hour of arriving back home.

"Mrs. Byard," the doctor said, "do you understand how serious this is?"

My mother appeared to not be dealing with it. As if she thought, I won't deal with it—it won't be there.

"Listen," Mom said, "I heard you. Let us handle this ourselves." She was annoyed; she had just been told her baby was dying, and she had to call Donald to tell him. Shirley was not having a good day.

I went into my room and listened through the walls as my mom and dad called Donald. No way was I getting on the phone with them. I wouldn't have known what to say. It would have been too uncomfortable. Too weird. The three of them—my "parents"—plotting to keep me from going back to school. I know I wasn't thinking clearly, and I know they were doing what they thought was best, but at the time I resented it, and I resented them. If there was ever any constant in my life, it was my desire to be a lawyer, and I was not going to allow some stupid growth to stop me.

School. In my head, I kept coming back to school. I stayed in my room all that afternoon and all night, and school was the only thing that made sense. It was where I belonged, what I should be doing. I wasn't about to let this rare and inoperable tumor keep me from where I was meant to be. (Who even heard of such a thing?) If I stayed home and submitted to my parents' wishes and the doctors' doomed course of radiation, I'd be beaten. I had to keep moving, I convinced myself. I had to go forward.

The next morning I stepped into the kitchen and made my position clear. "I'm going back to school," I said. "It means more to me than anything. There's no reason I can't have this radiation in Washington."

This time they listened, and after a good helping of tears and hugs and frantic phone calls to the hospital it was agreed. I would go down to Washington in the next few days, after I was feeling a little stronger, and the Trenton doctors would set me up with a radiologist at George Washington University Hospital, and we would just see how it went.

Now, from a more enlightened adult perspective, it's amazing to me that we put ourselves through all those paces on the strength of one medical opinion.

Granted, there was a team of doctors working on me in Trenton, but it was just *one* team, at *one* hospital. We should never have gone along with the stupid doctor's first opinion, but people believed in doctors back then. You didn't ask the kinds of questions you ask now. The doctor told me I had an inoperable tumor, so I had an inoperable tumor.

Still, I don't think I ever really thought I was going to die. Everyone around me thought I would die—it was all very clinical, and black and white, and right there—but I didn't process what was happening. How could I? I was twenty years old! No way was I dealing in any kind of reasoned manner with the concept of my own death. No matter what the doctors said, or my parents, it still wasn't part of my frame of reference.

I've since realized that this denial had more to do with my age and immaturity than my circumstance or resolve. At twenty, you're invincible, right? You never think about not being here. You think the world re- volves around you and that of course you will live forever because the world could not possibly go on without you. But by the same token, some young peo- ple don't fully appreciate what death is. When I started working in television years later, I reported a story about two young girls who had committed suicide. They were unhappy about something that happened at school and thought, Hey, let's just check out. What the hell is that? Check out? Check out to where? It's not like you can die, feel better about your situation, and then come back again. Death is final. Your earthly life is over. All those dreams about what career you will have?

Over. What kind of husband or wife you will be? Over. How many children you will have? Over.

It scares me now that some young people have such little regard for life, but I suppose that disregard flows from the same place as mine did, all those years ago. There's a difference, to be sure, but there's a connection. At twenty, I arrogantly thought that I couldn't die because I still had so much to do, and yet some young people today arrogantly think that death is something they can actually control. In recent months we have seen the reality of this on our televisions and in our newspapers far too often: young women not ready to be mothers, putting their newborn babies in toilets while continuing to party at a high school dance; young men who don't like the grades they receive, or whose girlfriends stop talking to them, or whose mothers forbid them to go to a party, taking guns to school and shooting everyone in sight. Dear God . . .

I truly think that when young people commit murder, they know what they're doing, but don't fully *understand* what they're doing. They can watch it on television. They can stand aside as someone is lowered into the ground, but it doesn't really register. I'm sorry, but it just doesn't. Death is what happens to your grandmother. It's not what happens to you, and when it hits you in the face you build up all your little defense mechanisms. That's what I did, in my own way, but I also saw the tragic results of such arrogance first-hand, as an attorney, and in the years since, I've often thought that my emotions, facing life-threatening surgery at the age of twenty, were much the same as the defendant's in one of the biggest murder cases I ever prosecuted. I've thought about this phenomenon long and hard, this youthful inability to fully understand and accept death, and that thinking has forever placed the facts of this one case squarely in the middle of my own memories. I can no longer revisit the time and place of my own brush with death without taking John Ball with me.

John Ball, an arrogant thirteen-year-old from the Gowanus housing projects in Brooklyn, grabbed his father's handgun and took it to the playground and shot a kid over a petty dispute. He shot him three times, basically because he thought the kid dissed him. Ball thought he'd heard him say something like, "If you weren't such a little boy, I'd knock you on your ass," and he went and got the gun and came back with it, meaning to blow the kid away. Only he got the wrong kid. The kid who'd loud-mouthed him had already left the scene, and Ball wound up shooting the boy's older brother by mistake.

Thirteen-year-olds today are different from when I was a kid. A lot's changed in just a couple generations. At thirteen, I still liked Barbie dolls. At thirteen, in some of the neighborhoods I had jurisdiction as a prosecutor, some girls were having their second baby. So it's very different. Now, a few years later, it's probably even worse. The average age of first experimentation for marijuana and cocaine is reaching down into the single digits in some communities. Can you believe it? Kids eight and nine years old smoking dope? I'm in my thirties, and I've never smoked a marijuana cigarette. (My cohost, Debbie, hates when I call it that. "It's a joint, Star," she says. "You should at least know what it's called, you big square.")

But that's what our world has become, and this kid John Ball was just a part of it. He came from an okay family. His mother was a social worker, his father a corrections officer. He was a bad kid, but he wasn't a criminal kid. He lived in a world where he thought you had to stand up and defend yourself if you were being disrespected. Talk about crap. A kid who had not lived long enough or achieved enough to be respected, kills someone because *he* was disrespected. I just wanted to shake him and tell him that he had disrespected himself by the act he committed.

The John Ball case really got to me. It was one of the reasons I left the district attorney's office. It was just too much to have to deal with, all the time. It was unrelenting. I was too young to have to seal the fate of a thirteen-year-old kid who couldn't possibly have understood what he was doing. Oh, he *knew* what he was doing, but he didn't get what it meant; he didn't understand that short-term decisions have long-term ramifications. I had him up on the stand during cross-examination, and he looked at me with such disdain and anger, as if this were something I was doing to him. And it wasn't just him. His sisters looked at me like I was the lowest form of life to walk the planet—a black woman prosecuting a black child as an adult, looking for the maximum. But this was not my fault. John Ball was responsible for his own situation. I couldn't help thinking that I wouldn't have had to deal with him at all if his family had given him a better sense of reality, if they'd done a better job. If they'd taught him that no one can make you a man and no one can take your manhood away. If he had received that from his family, he never would have gotten to me, there in that courtroom. In our house, we learned these things early on. It was basic. There was nothing that anyone could have said to me that would have reduced my self-esteem to the point where I would take a gun and take their life. You don't define how I see me. I define how I see me. And that comes from how I was raised.

The mother of the young man who was killed was there in court every day. I talked to her. One day she said to me, "I'm just waiting to see him afraid of what's happening to him. I need to see that he's scared." And I said, "You may never see it." And she never did, because it never fully registered on Ball what was happening, what he'd done. He knew, in his head, that we were hoping to put him away for life, but he didn't know it in his gut. He didn't know what it meant.

The defense attorney, Mitchell Dinnerstein, tried to sell the jury a line of liberal Brooklyn Heights crap that was so detrimental to us as a society, and to the kids involved, that I couldn't figure how this man could look at himself in the mirror. Dinnerstein did his summation first (the defense always goes first; I was the prosecutor, the one with the burden of proof), and he stood up and started in on how John Ball had been raised with a "ghetto mentality" that had nothing to do with him. It didn't start with him. It was bigger than him, this macho thing. It was the way he was taught to deal with being disrespected, to get his back up.

I swear, I don't think I'd ever been as angry at an

argument. I started to take it personally, because on the face of it the defense attorney was talking about me. When we first moved to Trenton, we lived in a housing project. My parents worked lower-income jobs. We're black. And yet we never had this so-called "ghetto mentality." We never bought into it, and I listened to this man's arguments and bristled. I thought, You're giving this kid an excuse to commit murder. He's thirteen and he's from the ghetto, so let him go. Give him a bye, a do-over, because he couldn't help himself; it was in his nature to do what he did. That was essentially his argument, and it was outrageous.

I tried never to prepare the beginning or opening remarks of my summations. I wrote out the facts, the guts of what I wanted to say, but I tried to play off what the other side was doing when I began, and that's what I did here. I had my copy of *The Rules of Criminal Procedure* with me, and the *Penal Code,* all the legal references we carried around with us, and the judge turned to me and said, "Miss Jones, would you care to sum up?" and I started paging furiously through these texts. There was a long pause, about thirty seconds or so. The judge asked me if I needed a break, some time to collect my thoughts, but I shook my head no. I'd made my point. I stood and faced the jury and explained: "You know," I said, "I just needed to take a moment there to look again, but for the life of me I cannot find the ghetto exception to murder in the laws of New York State. Maybe I should look again."

I had their attention, and I went on to talk about how I'd always been told that you may be born in the ghetto but the ghetto's not born in you. I talked about how we have decisions to make every single day. You can either turn to the left or turn to the right. It's up to you. It's called free will. And when you turn to the left, and you get a gun and point it at another human being and shoot and kill him, that's murder. In New York State, that's murder, whether you're thirteen or thirty. No matter where you were born, how you were raised, who your momma is, or who your daddy isn't. None of that has any relevance, not in this courtroom. Here, your actions represent who you are.

In the end, John Ball was convicted as an adult for murder (at the time I was one of the first prosecutors in New York State to ever get such a conviction) and sentenced to nine years to life in prison, and I don't remember feeling any grief over putting him away. The victim's mother came to the sentencing, and in one of the most moving recommendations to the court that I have ever heard she told the judge that God had given her her son, "to watch over his life," and she in turn had given him over to me, "to obtain justice for his death." And then I realized she had been holding something throughout the sentencing session. I hadn't noticed until just this moment, but when she finished her recommendation she stood and handed the object to me. It was an urn, containing the ashes of her murdered child. God, that nearly knocked me to the floor, and yet in that one moment I knew I'd done the right thing. Any sadness I felt at that sentencing I felt for the victim, and his mother.

If John Ball had shown some remorse, maybe I would have felt different, but he never showed any remorse. Sure, he was just a kid, but he took a life, even if he couldn't possibly have known what the taking of that life truly represented. Even if he couldn't know what his sentence would mean. And yeah, it took a piece of me to have to go through these motions, to see that justice was handed out, but I set this story out because it goes to my state of mind back in Trenton, back when I was just a kid myself. John Ball couldn't possibly have appreciated what he'd done, or what he was facing, because he wasn't conditioned to think in such absolute terms, and neither was I. Kids just don't think that way, and those who do can't know what to make of it. In my case, I ended up using my desperate situation to will myself to live; Ball used his as an excuse to kill. I knew it in my head, what was happening to me, but I didn't know it in my gut, and so I think I was able to find these tiny hiding places behind the truth and take comfort in my not fully knowing.

Stepping on someone else's sneakers is enough to get you killed in some parts of Brooklyn. Or looking the wrong way at the wrong person's girlfriend. These kids don't get that death is forever. It's why we see such a high suicide rate among teens, often as a result of some one-day problem that might have cleared itself up in another day or two. I hear all the time, when I lecture across the country, how ''my boy Joey was taken out in a drug deal gone bad,'' how ''Rashid ain't plannin' on bein' here in five years 'cause he'll probably be dead or in jail, but that's okay 'cause he's keepin' it real.'' What does that mean? Keepin' it real. It means keepin' real dead or real in jail.

I cringe when I come across this type of thinking from an adult perspective, but it didn't hit me, at twenty, that death was imminent. I didn't understand death. I didn't know what it meant to say to myself, "I'm gonna die." "Okay, Star, this is it." It just wasn't registering, in any kind of fundamental way, and that's the mind-set I took with me on my first visit to George Washington University Hospital to see about my radiation treatments. It was simply something I had to do—little different, in some respects, from a trip to the dentist or the dry cleaner.

I checked in at the hospital with a Lithuanian doctor who took one look at my charts and said, "You don't need radiation." He spoke in a thick accent. "Why do you take radiation? You need surgery."

Surgery? I thought, What planet have I just landed on? What is this guy talking about? "They told me the tumor was inoperable," I explained. (Can you believe I had to explain this? I barely understood it myself.)

"No," the doctor said dismissively, "they don't know what they're talking about." He gave me the name of a doctor—Benjamin Aaron, whom he called the best thoracic surgeon in the country. "You go see Dr. Aaron," the doctor said. "Tell him I sent you. Tell him you're here to start radiation."

I grabbed my chart and my X rays and marched upstairs to Dr. Aaron's office, where I found the man who would save my life stretched out with his feet up on his desk and his hands clasped behind his head, looking more like a health-club manager than a surgeon. He wore chinos and docksider shoes and an Izod shirt. "Let me see your pictures," the doctor said, extending his hand. He didn't get up to greet me, so I crossed the small office to his desk and handed him my

X rays. He looked at them briefly, and then, with all the arrogance I could ever pretend to have, announced that he would have this removed, if he were me.

"But they told me it was inoperable," I said, wanting to defend my position.

"For them, it is," he agreed, "but I can take this out."

"They said I was gonna die," I insisted. For some reason, I was holding on to the grim prospect that hadn't quite become a part of me in the two weeks since my diagnosis. I'd refused to accept it, but here I was reluctant to let it go. I felt like I was being tossed around like a rag doll, having to relinquish control of my life from one group of doctors to the next.

"You're not gonna die," the doctor assured me. "They were wrong. I'm right. Trust me."

I thought, Trust you? Why should I trust you over the other doctors I've already seen? I had all these bright, capable people telling me the tumor was inoperable, and now I was expected to believe they were wrong and this arrogant, Izod-wearing superdoctor knew something they didn't. What, they all missed the same class in medical school, while Mr. Big-time Dr. Aaron showed up and took notes?

He could see I was thrown, and that he had yet to make himself clear. "Look around the room," he said confidently. All around were framed photographs of Dr. Aaron with one dignitary or another. I noticed there were a whole bunch of pictures with Ronald Reagan.

"Great," I said, trying to match his arrogance.

"You're a Republican. Now I'm definitely not letting you at me with a scalpel."

He laughed, and explained that he was the doctor who took out President Reagan's bullet after he'd been shot. I thought, Okay, so maybe this guy *is* the best thoracic surgeon in the country. They don't let just anybody take bullets out of the president of the United States. So I asked him how it was that the other doctors had missed this, how he expected me to move from having an inoperable tumor to one that would be no trouble at all to remove.

"To be honest," he said, "it's not a simple tumor, and it's not the easiest procedure, but it can be done, and it's been done before." Unfortunately, he explained, it hadn't been done for the benefit of his current group of medical students at George Washington University Hospital, and since George Washington is a teaching hospital and this was such a rare situation, he would be able to put together the same team he used for the president and use my surgery as a teaching method for his students.

I thought, Cool. In fact, I was so caught up in thinking how cool it would be, to have the president's thoracic team working on me, Starlet Marie Jones, while a bunch of medical students looked on, that I lost for a moment the gift in what this man was telling me. Remember, I was still in my mortality-denial mode, so to go from the notion of having nine months to live to all of a sudden having all the time in the world wasn't as big a leap as you might think. The big deal was in having this world-class doctor perform a thymectomy on me in one of those cool teaching-theater operating rooms I'd only seen on television, with a world-class team of surgeons standing by to assist. Big-time cool. I was going to be operated on by the president's surgeon. Of course. Who else would be up to the job?

Dr. Aaron pulled me back to a more sensible view. "I want you to get a second opinion," he said.

"Jesus," I said, "who's gonna give me a second opinion? You just told me you're the best in the business."

Just the same, he set up an immediate appointment with a colleague, Dr. Kashishian. The man's office was just a few blocks away, and I hurried over there with my charts and my X rays, thinking, Here we go again with the damn X rays.

I handed the film to Dr. Kashishian, and the man barely looked up when he spoke. Apparently, there's this thing among thoracic surgeons about not looking up at their patients when they first meet. "Ben Aaron is the best," Dr. Kashishian said, finally meeting my eyes. "He'll take it out. I'll assist."

Dr. Kashishian told me I didn't have to worry about a thing, but there were a few things I was worried about, actually. For one, my parents. They were so torn up about my decision to go back to school, I was afraid they wouldn't see this opportunity for what it was. They'd probably think I was refusing to accept the reality of my prognosis, or that I wasn't up to the radiation treatments. For another, I was worrying how we would pay for such a high-risk, high-end procedure. Surely the president's thoracic team was beyond the reach of my medical coverage.

We went back to Ben's office to sort through the

details, and call my folks, and see about admitting me and scheduling the procedure. In the middle of all this, I realized I'd started to call Dr. Aaron by his first name. Here's this major megaguy and I'm calling him Ben.

Now, this was on a Monday, the first day of classes. I'd set up the initial radiation appointment for the afternoon, so I wouldn't have to miss classes and I'd have the chance to rest that evening before going back to classes on Tuesday. But now my thoracic team wanted to check me in on Tuesday and do the surgery on Wednesday, so everything was moving pretty fast. My mother, predictably, flipped out.

"What are you talking about, Starlet?" she shot back over the phone. It was as if I'd told her I'd renounced the radiation treatments in favor of a mud bath. "You get back in there and take those treatments like we agreed."

"Mom," I said, trying to calm her down but firm in my decision. "I'm having the surgery. These people know what they're doing. You can either come and sit with me and hold my hand, or you can stay there and yell."

Just then, my new friend Ben took the phone from me and introduced himself to my mother. He explained who he was, what he'd found, and what he thought he could do for me. After five minutes, my mother was as comfortable with him as I was, and she was climbing into the car to drive down to Washington to be at my side.

I look back on that crazy, whirlwind day and think what a little horror show I must have been, to make a decision like that without involving my parents. Really,

I was just such a little know-it-all, and it's no wonder my mother was flipping out, but I believe my audacity had mostly to do with not really thinking about my situation.

Still, it was the right choice, the only choice, and my parents could see that. And anyway, how could they be mad at me? They thought they'd lose me within the year, and if all went well with the surgery they'd be stuck with me, so I suppose they were willing to forgive a little headstrong behavior in exchange for a longer-term prognosis.

My entire family came down to the hospital—and I do mean my entire family. My parents. My grandparents. (Mama Muriel and Daddy Paul had passed on before I graduated high school, but my grandma Pauline and my granddaddy Clyde made the trip.) Eight aunts. Even Donald came. I didn't see them all, before the operation, but I knew they were there, and I knew that if they were all there this was serious stuff. I knew there were risks. Ben told me I might not wake up. It was an eight-hour procedure, and there are risks involved in any major surgery, but the longer you're on the table the greater the chance that something might go wrong. Plus, in my case, they were removing this huge mass that had wrapped itself around my esophagus, any portion of which could have been cancerous, and if it was, and it came in contact with any other organs, the cancer might have spread.

By Wednesday morning I was scared. For the first time in my life. I lay there while they prepped me for surgery and started singing an old spiritual my Mama Muriel used to sing to me when I was little. I hadn't realized I even remembered the words, but the song just came out:

I don't feel no ways tired;
I've come too far from where I started from;
Nobody told me the road would be easy;
But I don't believe He brought me this far to leave me.

I sang it to myself, in my head at first and then quietly, in a whisper, and it relaxed me. I was singing when they wheeled me into the operating theater, and it occurred to me it was like a scene in a movie. I was Mahalia Jackson in *Imitation of Life,* as they bring the poor dead woman out on the street. I was being wheeled into surgery and this is what was running through my head, Mahalia Jackson and this old spiritual. I got myself all worked up. My body was no problem, but my head was beginning to freak out. I looked up at all the students filing into the viewing area, and I lost it. I wasn't going through with it, I decided. I couldn't. I had no idea what'd come over me, or where it'd come from, but I started to kick and fuss, to where the nurses went and summoned Ben.

Realize, most surgeons don't like to see their patients in the operating room just before major surgery; they wait until they're out of it, but Ben came in and asked me what the problem was.

"To hell with it," I said. "I've changed my mind. I'm not doing it."

"What's the problem?" he asked again.

I looked up at all those students looking down on me. "The people," I said.

"Star," he said, "you knew there were going to be students watching. We talked about this."

"Yes, but I'm still awake. I can see them." I looked down at my chest, which was all exposed. "And they can see me. Once I'm out of it, I don't care, but I can't have them here now."

He understood, and cleared the operating theater. The students didn't know what was going on, but if Ben Aaron told them to leave the room, they left the room.

"That better?" he said.

I nodded.

He asked if I wanted him to stay with me while they put me to sleep, and I nodded again. The last thing he said to me, before I dropped off, was this: "Just remember, Star. I'm going to save your life, and you're going to be a very famous lawyer someday, and you will never sue doctors."

He was right. I am. And I never have. (That's for you, Ben—you arrogant genius whom I love as much as I love my own family.)

The surgery itself ran longer than expected, but it was for the most part uneventful. Ben unraveled the tumor and removed it slowly, painstakingly, and then they sent me off to the recovery room. That's the next thing I remember. When you're waking from a deep sleep, under anesthesia, there's a moment in there when your brain is working ahead of everything else. That's how it was for me. I could hear people talking, all the noises in the room, but I was too tired to open my eyes or my mouth. I could hear the *beep, beep, beep* of all the machines. I could hear this one extralong *beeeeeeeep,* and then I could hear the machines go silent, and I thought to myself, I'm not dead. I hope they know I'm not dead. Is this dead? This can't be dead. And then I heard a crisp clapping of hands, and a nurse's voice saying, "Wake up, Star. Wake up!" And then I could feel someone slapping my feet, and I was trying to summon the strength to tell these people I was still alive and to leave my feet alone. This saccharine-sweet voice kept telling me to wake up, and someone kept hitting me on the feet, and I thought, I wish this nurse would stop hitting me on my damn feet. And then I heard laughter, and my mother's voice saying, "She's gonna be fine."

It turned out that whatever I was thinking was also coming out of my mouth. They heard it all—me insisting I wasn't dead, me telling the nurse to stop hitting me, everything—and by the time I opened my eyes and figured out what was going on, they were all laughing and smiling. My mother was there, and Daddy, and my little sister, and they were all just so glad to see me, and I was just so incredibly glad to be seen. For the next few days I'd catch my mother looking at me behind one of her patented crying-smiles, and I'd try not to break down myself. Daddy told me later how she'd come in the room and brush my hair and smile and be so happy, and then she'd go out to have a cigarette and start to cry hysterically, because of what she'd almost lost—because of what we'd all almost lost.

I wound up missing only a week of school. I had to go through eight weeks of radiation, just as a precaution, but Ben helped me set it up so it wouldn't interfere with classes. And my whole life changed in that one week I spent recuperating. My mother and Donald saw each other for the first time in years, and managed not to kill each other—and I fell in love with my daddy, Jimmy. Whenever you read "Daddy," or hear me say "Daddy" that's who I'm talking about. He's earned that title several times over. After the surgery, he stepped in and lifted my soul when I was about as low as a person could be. See, one of the things I hadn't counted on was the scar Ben would have to leave behind. He did the best he could, but there would still be a big scar running down my chest, and even though I'd been prepped intellectually to accept or anticipate this scar, I wasn't dealing with it too well. Before the surgery, I'd had a gold medal–winning chest—the boobs of life!—truly, two for the archives. I was a 42DD. I wore low-cut, cleavage-advertising clothes, because I always thought, Hey, if you've got it, honey, you might as well strut. I was solid—about 165 pounds—but I used to joke that most of it was chest, and I flaunted my abundant gifts. I thought it was one of the features that made me attractive, and determined my worth as a woman, and all that nonsense, and when the time came to take off the bandages and see what the scar looked like I was frantic. The plan was for my mother to be with me, but I couldn't stand waiting once the nurses came in to start unwrapping, so my dad pinch-hit for her. And he nailed it.

I asked for a mirror and saw the scar for the first time. And the tears came. I said, "Daddy, no man is ever going to look at me again. With this scar, no man will ever want me."

"Princess," he said, seeing that I was devastated by the ugly scar on my perfect chest. "Don't you even worry about it. The way you're built, the brothers ain't lookin' at that scar."

I turned to that dear, sweet man, who'd somehow managed to come up with the exact right thing to say, and I kissed him. And I cried. And sure enough, the first time I was with a guy after the operation, he didn't even notice, and I just had to call my daddy and tell him. The guy I was with must have thought I was kinda strange, to be reaching for the phone to call my father with a report on our lovemaking, but I just had to tell him that he was right and I was fine and everything was gonna be okay.

So, what did I learn from all this? Where did it take me? Well, naturally I've learned never to take anything for granted. And always get a second opinion. But more than this, it's redirected my entire outlook on life. I came out of that ordeal a driven young woman. I'd always been a positive person, and I'd always gone after what I wanted, but now it came into such focus that my motivation increased exponentially. All of a sudden, my life had a purpose. There wasn't just a reason to get out of bed each morning and go to class and study hard; there was every reason. And I would do all these things with a kind of immunity. Stuff would happen all around me—a car accident, or a plane crash, or an earthquake —and I'd know in my heart it was not my time. I'd know He kept me here for a reason, and that I wasn't going anywhere until I figured it out, because, let's face it, there's no reason that I should still be alive. None whatsoever. And now, here it is my job to go down a purposeful path, and to keep on that path, no matter what.

Absolutely, He kept me here for a reason. And I don't believe He brought me this far to leave me.

Stabbing Myself

❧

When you know better, you do better.

—MAYA ANGELOU

I LANDED MY job in the district attorney's office fairly early on, at the beginning of my third and final year of law school. I was offered the position in October, and I took it in November, and it was there waiting for me when I got my degree the following May.

That last semester was a great coast. I knew I had a gig. I knew that all I had to do was start preparing for the bar exam and pass all my remaining classes—no small task, but I wasn't exactly feeling any front-burner pressure, if you know what I mean. It was probably the first (and, come to think of it, the last) time in my life when my course was determined, and the only thing left was to wait for the calendar to give me the go-ahead.

So there I was, itching to get started, and for that whole year I kept wishing time would just hurry up and get on with it. I remember it like a transition scene from a bad movie, with the pages of a calendar flipping against the backdrop of the changing seasons. Believe me, honey, those pages couldn't flip fast enough. Finally, the calendar landed on the rest of my life, and I showed up in court for the very first time. One of the judges had a senior assistant district attorney bring me into his courtroom, and for the life of me I couldn't figure out why. Had I done something wrong? Already? I'd just gotten there, and right away I was being called in to see the judge for what I thought would be a dressing-down.

"I'm sorry to pull you in like this, Miss Jones," the judge said when I arrived, "but I wanted to meet the woman whose mother named her Starlet."

I laughed loud enough to cover my sigh of relief, and I thought, This is gonna be okay. It was a real watershed moment, as if the skies parted to announce my arrival, and to make room. As much as I'd wanted this career, as hard as I'd worked for it and as long as I'd dreamed of it, I was still pretty anxious over how I'd do. Law school was one thing, but this was the real deal. And yet here, in this very human exchange with a kind judge, I was able to sense some possibilities. I could start to see a fit, and where I might make my mark.

From that day forward, nothing filled me with a greater sense of pride or a bigger surge of good feeling than to stand in that judge's courtroom and declare, "Starlet Jones for the People of the State of New York." It was a ringing validation of everything I'd set out to achieve, echoing through every working day. It's not every job that allows you to stand up and shout out your name and state your agenda. (Beauty pageant contestant comes to mind, but it's not quite the same thing, is it?) I always thought it was kinda cool—a gentle, daily reminder of who I was and what I was doing with my life. Goodness, it still rings with all kinds of bravado and purpose and wonder. "Star Jones for the People." I don't think I'll ever lose the weight of those words, or what they meant to a twenty-four-year-old kid, fresh out of law school. The privilege of saying them was worth the entire ride—and they made the not knowing where the ride would take me all the more thrilling.

I made some serious noise right away. Along with the bravado, purpose, and wonder came a significant dose of arrogance. Among the baby assistant DAs, as we called ourselves, I was one of the first to try a case (and, resultantly, one of the first to win a case), one of the first to pass the bar, and one of the first to go up against a heavy-hitter defense attorney. I tallied up these firsts like they were hard currency. It was important to me to get a jump-start on things, maybe a little too important. The judges didn't quite know what to make of me, but most seemed to like me enough to allow me a little rope. The same was true with my superiors in the office. Even my contemporaries weren't sure what to think of my extra efforts. They all knew they had to deal with me, but I'm not sure they knew how. I was an interesting, driven character, not at all like the other rookies in the office. I even dressed differently, sort of like a wannabe "lady who lunches," with the pearls and the pumps and the Chanel jackets.

(Aw, who am I kidding? What I *really* wore were those Chanel knockoffs, which I picked up on Canal Street in lower Manhattan and accessorized with fake Chanel buttons, which I sewed on myself. Hey, a girl's gotta do what a girl's gotta do.)

With each day, I started to move about the office with more and more confidence. The courtroom, too. I tried a second case. I started to get full of myself, and I'll confess I wasn't shy about trumpeting my accomplishments. I'm sure you've heard the saying, "Be kind to the people you meet on the way up, because you'll meet them again on the way down." Well, it might have been coined with me in mind. It wasn't that I was unkind to any of my new colleagues, but I put a little too much emphasis on my own agenda. I didn't recognize this at the time (people who are so full of themselves rarely see things as they are in the unfolding), but I saw it soon enough. I was determined not only to be a good assistant district attorney, but also to be the best, brightest, and boldest assistant district attorney Brooklyn had ever seen, and every professional choice I made had in some way to do with that goal. I didn't step on people, but I did step over them if they were in my way. It wasn't a cold calculation so much as a part of who I was. I didn't have it in me to do any less.

Finally, just a few months into the job, I caught a

case I thought might propel me to the next level. A well-known rap artist was accused of stabbing his ex-girlfriend's new boyfriend. It was a typical Brooklyn thing: Boy gets girl; boy loses girl; boy stabs girl's new boyfriend. Only in Brooklyn, right? It was the highest-profile misdemeanor case to appear on the docket, and at that stage in my career—after I'd taken the bar exam but was still awaiting the results—I was not yet allowed to try felonies. Borderline misdemeanors were about the best I could hope for, and this was about the best borderline misdemeanor I could imagine. As a matter of fact, when the stabbing case came in, the initial charge was attempted murder, on the theory that a knife wound to the chest is usually inflicted with the intent to kill, but by the time I checked in, it had been knocked down to assault three. (Once again, only in Brooklyn could a knife wound to the chest be considered a misdemeanor.)

I knew that if I won this case, which at the time was the focus of a sliver of media attention, I'd be the star of my incoming class, and for the first time in my just-getting-started career I allowed my desire to win to cloud my good judgment. Mercifully, it was also the last. What happened, essentially, was that I put myself in a position where my integrity was called into question. It was only my third trial and I was so desperate to win, for so many wrong reasons, that I cut corners. I got too close to my witness, and to the victim. I made it personal.

Looking back, I think I enjoyed the way I looked in the eyes of the victim and his girlfriend. They were just young kids—nineteen years old—and I wasn't much older, and I liked that they looked at me as the one with the influence, the one with the power. I liked the "juice" of that image, and I bought into it myself, and in the process I lost sight of what I was there to do. I didn't do anything sneaky, mind you, just foolish. I went out to dinner with these two kids. They came over to my apartment. We went nightclubbing.

One of the first things you learn as an attorney is not just to avoid impropriety, but to avoid the *appearance* of impropriety, and yet here I crossed the line. I mean, to befriend a witness and a victim? It wasn't unheard of, but the way I went about it was certainly unprofessional. I allowed myself to move from an advocate for a certain position to an adversary. A lot of people consider your opponent to be your adversary, but as a prosecuting attorney I was an advocate for a position. It wasn't me against the defendant. It was me standing on behalf of the community against what that defendant allegedly did. There's a difference. It was completely improper and unprofessional for me to allow the case to become about exacting some kind of revenge on behalf of my two young friends. But that's what I did. I made it all about me, and how I looked to these two young kids, and winning at all costs.

Well, my foolishness came back to bite me—in the ass and in the courtroom; the defense attorney made sure of that. I was seen with the victim and the witness at a nightclub, and it was introduced in such a way as to suggest I was having some sort of intimate relationship with the victim. I couldn't believe it, although I should have seen it coming. Yeah, it was an improper relationship, but it wasn't a sexual relationship. I wasn't that stupid. Still, I left myself open to the charge, and that's what counted. The defense attorney's line of questioning had everything to do with how many times the victim had dinner in Miss Jones's home, or whether or not we'd spent evenings alone together. I was mortified. Had I been on that jury, I would have thought, Yes, Star Jones crossed the line. Yes, she dropped the ball. It's taken me years to admit it, but that's what I would have thought. The defense attorney was right to make it an issue, and I was wrong to give him the ammunition. My credibility was rightly called into question. The witness's credibility was rightly called into question. The facts of the case based on that witness's credibility were rightly called into question, and the jury returned the correct verdict based on how I allowed the trial to play out. It was not the just verdict, and yet justice was served. If I couldn't prove the defendant's guilt beyond a reasonable doubt, then the jury was obligated to say he was not guilty, and I certainly gave them more than a little room for doubt.

Let me tell you a little something about reasonable doubt. It's not what you *think* happened based on your gut instinct. It's what you can *prove* based on the evidence. Any one fact or any group of facts can tilt the scales against the prosecution . . . and rightly so. There's no question in my mind, still, that we had the right guy. This rap artist did what he was charged with doing. But he wasn't punished because I screwed up. The jury came back with a not-guilty verdict, and I was publicly humiliated. That's what happens, I learned, when prosecutors don't do their jobs: Guilty people go free. I felt like crawling in a hole and disappearing for a good long time. (Years later, another female prosecutor would screw up a much bigger case, on a much bigger stage, and out of that mess land a multimillion-dollar book deal. Talk about falling *up*. But that's for another book.)

Of course, me being the arrogant person who put herself in this position in the first place, I blamed the defense attorney for humiliating me. It was his fault, I told anyone who would listen, not mine. He crossed the line. He made the case about me. He tripped me up and made me look ridiculous. I may have shown some poor judgment, and I might have done things differently if I had them to do over again, but I didn't really do anything *that* wrong.

Oh, but I did. I was just too cocky to admit it, back then. There was no reason for me to be spending so much time with these two kids, except to feed my own ego. I could have gotten what I needed from them to try the case in a couple sessions in my office. If I wanted them to relax and feel comfortable around me, so that they might feel comfortable on the stand in court, I could have achieved these things with a few long walks, on a crowded street, in the light of day. But it was the smugness of youth and inexperience—*my* youth and *my* inexperience—that left me feeling I could deal with these kids however I wanted, and it cost me the case and a couple pounds of my reputation and more than a few nights' sleep.

Thank God I made these mistakes when I did, three months into my career, and not later on, when the stakes were higher. At some later point, it could have crushed me. As it was, it was pretty horrible back in the office. There were whispers. I'd been flying so high that there were a few people happy to see me shot down in such a public way. It's not like I messed up in private; this was a court of law; people's lives were at stake. There were more folks mumbling that I'd gotten what I deserved than there were folks rallying to my defense. It had been so important to me to be without peer in that office, that here I was left nakedly vulnerable. Without peer. There was no one to turn to, no place to look for moral support outside my family, and they couldn't know what was really going on. It was absolutely the lowest point of my young adulthood, and for a while there I wondered if I'd ever get my reputation back, if I'd ever fly as high as I'd been during those first few months.

Apparently, I wasn't the only person wondering what my career had in store. A few days into this fallout I heard from a woman who would stand as a real guardian angel in the months ahead. Kathy Plaszner Belson was, without question, the best female trial attorney I've ever seen in front of a jury. (I include myself in this equation, arrogantly enough, but Kathy was even better than me.) She could walk jurors through a string of complicated events as plainly as if they'd been there themselves. She could pull all the right strings and hit all the right notes and anticipate all the right angles. And yet she too had been crucified in the Brooklyn DA's office for her handling of one particular trial, early in her career. Her screwup was a little more prominent than mine, and she was crucified in the New York press as well, but she knew what I was going through. We knew each other from around the office—

Kathy worked in the homicide division—and I think she saw a little of herself in me. I was a Young Turk kid lawyer, same as she had been, flying a little too high, a little too soon. She came to me one day and said, "Star, you have talent, and you'll get through this." She told me that I had "erred on the side of arrogance," and that the silver lining was that I wouldn't make the same mistake again.

She and her partner in the homicide division, Jerry Green, one of the best and most compassionate lawyers I've ever met, took me under their wings and got me through this most difficult time. I'd known them both, but mostly by reputation, so it really was the kindness of strangers. They didn't have to reach out to me, but they did, and it made all the difference. I folded like a little dove in their hands, and let them guide me in the right direction. I was about as low as a person could be in the two months following the trial, but Kathy and Jerry were there with some reasoned words of encouragement each and every day. "You'll learn from this." "Grow." "Move on." "Put it behind you." "Don't ever forget that this is what you are meant to do."

There was snickering behind my back. There was finger pointing. There was even a mini-investigation. The most difficult piece, really, was the snickering and snide commentary from the other baby DAs, and the fact that my witness and the victim were now looking to comfort me. My, how those tables had turned!

It was during these two months that I learned I'd passed the bar on the first shot, and I was sworn in, but even these happy developments couldn't chase the funk I was in. All those little clichés that you tell yourself when you screw up didn't seem to work. *Pick yourself up and dust yourself off.* What the hell was that? They didn't work because I didn't believe them, and I didn't believe in me. I was too down to lift myself up on someone else's support. It had to come from me. I had to learn to forgive myself. I knew what my potential was. I knew what this mistake was costing me. I looked at myself in the mirror and didn't like the reflection that came back. I was ashamed. I'd disappointed my superiors. I'd disappointed the victim and my witness. And perhaps worst of all, I'd disappointed myself. I could have won that case with my eyes closed. Still could, to this day. But I lost the case with my eyes wide open and my head on backward and my priorities all out of whack.

Gradually, though, Kathy and Jerry pulled me back to a long-term view. Yes, I screwed up, but people screw up all the time, they reminded me. The key is to learn from your mistakes and work to never repeat them. And, indeed, it taught me the best lesson. I did everything in my power, from that point on, to always be on the right side. I never came close to faltering again, and I wound up being promoted when I was supposed to be promoted, and put back in the spotlight when I was meant to be back in the spotlight. I may have lost a stride or two with my misstep, but soon enough I was catching the right cases and making the best of them and was once again on a fast track to the next level.

What I learned from all this is there's a fine line between confidence and arrogance. I'm sure there are people all around me who think I'm arrogant—then and still—but I know what arrogance is, and I know when I get close to that line. I've experienced it, and I know what it can cost me, so I don't come close to it anymore. I can't. It's no longer in me. With the law, it was easy to steer clear. I knew that I could effect change if I remained true to the principles of the law. The experience didn't leave me a cold, hardened person, as it might have without the patient intervention of people like Kathy and Jerry. Rather, it left me warmer, more responsive—with a little less arrogance and a lot more humility. At least, that's what I was shooting for, and I don't believe I'm too far off the mark. It was a true wake-up call, and it reminded me full in the face what I was doing in the district attorney's office in the first place. It wasn't about being a star. It wasn't about holding the jury in the palm of my hand. It wasn't about showing off in front of an impressionable witness and victim. It wasn't even about winning.

What it was about, in the end, was being the only person standing between justice and injustice. For this small period of time, for this one case, whatever case it was, whatever the circumstances, it was all on me, and I wasn't about to let my immaturity catch me sleeping a second time. No way.

Who You Gonna Get to Drive the Bronco?

∽

The loneliest woman in the world is a woman
without a close woman friend.

—TONI MORRISON

THIS IS NOT about O. J. Simpson. (Gotcha!) But seriously, this is just not the place for an examination of the "trial of the century." That's for another book. I can, however, use Simpson and his circumstances to make a point, and that point is this:

I don't care if you think O. J. Simpson is a vicious, coldhearted murderer, a narcissistic jock who got what he deserved or a misunderstood man run through our criminal justice system on a raw ride. Say what you will, but the man could make a friend. Millions of people were lining up to lynch this man, and yet he had his good friends in his corner from the beginning. Talk about true friends. None were truer than Al Cowlings. I know it sounds weird, but whenever I think of true friendship I keep coming back to that night in June 1994, watching that now-famous Bronco chase on live television. What that man did, putting his own life on the line like that, was the ultimate sign of friendship, and it set me to wondering, Who would be my Al Cowlings? Who would drive the Bronco for me?

We all need an A. C. in our life, and we all need to be an A. C. to someone else. For me, nothing is more important. Sure, I understand a lot of people look at Al Cowlings's actions as a kind of ego play. They say he wasn't thinking straight, that he couldn't see clearly through the spotlight, that the heroism he showed (if that's what you want to call it) was mixed with some messed-up notions of power and privilege and posturing. But I don't see it that way. I've met Al Cowlings, and we've talked a little bit about that night, and my instincts tell me that for him, that long, uncertain ride was about friendship, just.

As it happened, I watched that Bronco ride with my own A. C., Vanessa Bell Calloway. We were at her in-laws' home in Los Angeles, enjoying one of the best views in the city and an NBA playoff game on the big-screen television. Fred and Jeannie Calloway were like my adopted godparents, and their house had become my home away from home after I moved to L.A. to do my own talk show, *Jones & Jury*. Every holiday, every major sporting event, every Sunday afternoon with nothing else to do, their friends, and their kids' friends, all seemed to gravitate to Fred and Jeannie's house. There we were, watching the game, not knowing whether the transplanted New Yorkers had more of a rooting interest in the Knicks than my friend Lita had in the Houston Rockets. (See, Lita and I went to law school in Houston together, and she had at one time been engaged to Hakeem Olajuwon, the great Houston center, and together they had a daughter—my godchild Abi!—so our allegiance was a little bit all over the place.)

Anyway, during the time-outs, I would check in with my big-mouth commentary on what had been going on in the Simpson case. Remember, even before the Bronco ride, all anybody wanted to talk about was the Simpson case, especially out in Los Angeles. Everyone was speculating on Simpson's role in the double murder of Ronald Goldman and Nicole Brown Simpson just days before. I was one of the few people in the room who'd never met O. J. Simpson, and yet for some reason my friends were looking to me as a kind of authority on the man's business, given my recent career spins as a prosecutor-turned–legal commentator-turned–legal talk show host.

As you might imagine, I wasn't shy about giving my opinion. There was a lot to consider. That morning, the talk in the newspapers was of a deal for Simpson to surrender himself for arrest, and by the afternoon he was nowhere to be found. The Los Angeles Police Department was embarrassed, and furious at Simpson's attorney, Robert Shapiro, for allowing the situation to unravel. "Only in America," I said, as our conversation turned back to the case, "can a rich black man be allowed to turn himself in when he's accused of killing two white people. And only in America can we then go and lose his ass before we get him into custody."

"Aw, Star," someone muttered. "You don't mean that."

"No, baby, I do," I insisted. "I absolutely do."

In another place, at another time, folks would have taken O. J. out to the nearest tree, just on the allegation that he had killed two white people, and if it turned out they were wrong about his involvement, well, then that would just be too bad. The mere fact that he'd been allowed to turn himself in tells you something about the power of celebrity in our society; regardless of money or race, it is, perhaps, the only currency that can spare you the indignity of a public arrest.

Then came the bulletin about the Bronco, and live pictures from the 405, and Simpson's friend Robert Kardashian reading what may or may not have been a suicide note, and I sat there wondering if we had somehow flipped to *All My Children*. I mean, really, nothing like this had ever happened to my girl Erica Kane (except perhaps for the season when she kidnapped the baby). All day, I'd been "holding court," as my friends would say, explaining the whats, wheres, and hows of what was happening. I thought I knew everything, until all of a sudden I was struck dumb. We all were. We sat there like idiots, waiting to be told what was happening, what planet we were living on. If you could have pulled a camera back and taken a picture of all of us, the expression on our faces would have been one giant "Huh?"

On NBC, they switched the basketball game to a picture-in-a-picture broadcast, with the white Bronco in the tiny box at the bottom of the screen, and then they switched it so that it was the other way around, with the game in miniature, and I knew enough about the television business to know that some news executive, somewhere, was growing an ulcer the size of the Bronco itself. I remember thinking we were all in the middle of something profoundly important—or, at least, something we would talk about for years to come. Yes, it was absurd and out there and unfathomable, but we were all fixed on it. Even the ones who were pissed about missing the game were glued to the screen, and what struck us, I think, was the sheer surprise of it, the shock of the new. It was great human drama, but we had no frame of reference for what was going on, and no idea where it would take us.

When we started hearing about Al Cowlings, and who he was and what his relationship with O. J. Simpson was about, the talk among our group turned naturally to friendship. It was clear to all of us that Cowlings must have been a great friend to Simpson, because every police officer in Los Angeles was on his tail (or just about), and any one of them could have lost his head at any time during this strange ordeal. Yet here was this man willing to put his life on the line for his friend. His life, his reputation, everything. Let me tell you something: Ever since that night, that image has stood as the picture of friendship. For me, that's what it all comes down to—A. C. leading that slow caravan along the 405, his best friend in the backseat with a gun to his head, an unimaginable craziness in their wake, and no one knowing anyone else's next move. Baby, that's friendship. That's the kind of friend I want to be, and the kind of friend I want in my corner.

I would drive the Bronco for my friend Vanessa in a minute, and for me that's saying a lot. I mean, I'm Little Miss Law and Order. I believe in following the rules, and paying the price for our transgressions, but I also think there are certain things that are more important than anything else. Friendship. Devotion. Trust. If Vanessa needed me, I'd be there for her. No matter what. No matter the consequences. No matter the circumstances. No matter. If she's in trouble, I'm there. I would drive that Bronco. I'd risk everything I'd worked my whole life to achieve, and I'd do it gladly, without hesitation. And I go to bed knowing she'd do the same for me. That's a cool feeling, and it's different from the ways we tend to feel about our own families. Naturally, I'd put myself out there for my mom or my dad or my sister. They wouldn't even have to ask. But you don't choose your family. You choose your friends, and they choose you, and that's all the difference in the world.

Would I lie in court? Hmmm. No, I would not. I wouldn't even lie to protect my own mother. She wouldn't expect me to—and more important, she'd be ashamed of me if I did. But for some reason, true friendship cuts nearly as deep as the law in my book, and I suppose I can never be sure what I wouldn't do on Vanessa's behalf, or what I wouldn't ask her to do on mine. (Mind you, all of this is in theory, because my girl Vanessa is a big chicken who would never do anything illegal in the first place.)

We trust each other, Vanessa and me, and that has to

be at the core of any good friendship. Once that trust is gone, honey, so am I, but it's all there at the outset. You come into my life, I presume you're a good person. But when you screw up, I start building walls, and after that it's almost impossible to tear them back down. I like to think I'm a very forgiving person, but I don't forget. As a result, what winds up happening is I let a whole lot of people into my life, which is a good thing, but then there are more people around to disappoint you, which isn't a good thing at all. Still, it's the only way I know to be, and I'll go on trusting people completely until they give me a reason not to.

I'm one of those people with little collections of friends in different pockets. These days, I have a core group of girlfriends: Vanessa, Lela, Lita, Holly, and Cheryl. They're my hanging partners. I have my great new work friends—Barbara Walters, Meredith Vieira, Debbie Matenopolous, and Joy Behar—and I truly treasure the lifelong friendships we've set about building. I have my other L.A. friends—Allison, Vivica, Jackee, LaTanya, and Anna Marie. I have my college roommate, Ladonna, with whom I pledged my sorority. I have my law school friends, Deidre and Detra, and Detra's husband Ricky. I have my former assistant and dear friend Susan Esterhay. I have my New York friends, Marva, Denise, Bernadette, Mike, and David. I have my confidante Raemali in Boca Raton who I'd walk over hot coals for. And I have my boys—Leo, Tony, Sam, Elgin, Kevin, Leonard, Rodney, and Rodney. (Phew!) Okay, so I have good friends all over the place, but it's Vanessa, Lela, Lita, Holly, and Cheryl at the center of my life. That's my circle. They're the ones who get the call whenever I'm coming to Los Angeles. They're the ones I can ring up in the middle of the night—for good reason, or no reason at all. They're the ones who show up at my hotel room, unannounced and uninvited, the morning the Emmy nominations are reported. They heard on the news that *The View* was nominated, and they obviously knew I was, in town, and they just blew off whatever it was they had to do to come and celebrate with me. I mean, these are professional, career-oriented, busy women (lawyers, actresses, mothers), but nothing was a bigger deal to them at just that moment than what was happening for their friend. So that's my crowd, and now that I'm in New York I miss 'em like crazy.

But I never really processed the depths of our friendships until that night, watching A. C. do his thing on the television. I looked at the television, at this person with a gun to his head, and this other person driving and frantically talking on the cellular telephone, and I asked myself, If I were the person with the gun to her head, who would drive the Bronco? Vanessa. My best friend. She'd drive for me, and I'd drive for her.

It's the true measure of a friendship, don't you think? I suppose some people would suggest that the better sign of a true friend is someone who'll never let your ass get into such a desperate position in the first place, but I don't believe we can police our friends any more than we can police ourselves. In the end, we all make our own decisions, and bear responsibility for our own actions, but it's the folks who bail us out who count on this score. It's the Al Cowlingses and the Vanessa Bell Calloways who make our lives meaningful, and when you can stand in the same place for someone else it's most meaningful of all. At least that's how it resonates for me.

You know, it's funny, but with Vanessa it took about an hour before I knew we'd be friends for the next million years. We met at a sorority event in Los Angeles. She had pledged an Alpha Kappa Alpha chapter in Ohio. I was a sister at American University in Washington, D.C. I was attending the event as one of AKA's former national vice presidents. Vanessa was a featured guest, as one of our better-known alumnae. (She's an actress, my friend Vanessa; you'd recognize her immediately: *What's Love Got to Do With It?; Daylight,* with Sylvester Stallone; *Crimson Tide,* with Denzel Washington; and one of my favorite shows, *All My Children.*) There were five or six thousand women at this convention—all of them bright, successful, accomplished people, and quite a few of them were clamoring for Vanessa's attention. I wasn't quite clamoring, but I was a fan and made an effort to meet her. We shook hands and said hello and within an hour we were ducking out to have a drink and take in a movie. We just clicked right away, and we've been best friends ever since. We've known each other for so long and been through so much that we actually measure our friendship by the kinds of champagne we've drunk over the years—the labels and quality changed as our success and friendship grew. We started with Cook's, went to Korbel and Piper-Sonoma, graduated to Mumm's, Moët, and Dom or Cristal on special occasions, and now have settled in with Veuve Clicquot for every day and Taittinger Rosé when we celebrate. That's my girl.

When we first met, she was getting married in a couple of months, and she went home that very night and said to her fiancé, "Tony, I met my girl." And he said, "All right, let's go to dinner." And that's what we did. The very next night, we all canceled our plans so we could hang out and get to know each other, and Tony signed on to the deal straightaway.

Vanessa's husband, Dr. Anthony Calloway, is the man most women dream about as the perfect mate. He is a smart, handsome, and loving anesthesiologist. (I told you she had it going on!) Vanessa always says she knew he was the one for her when he helped her take out her "weave" one night. Her favorite line is, "I want a man who will love me in between touch-ups." They have two little girls—Ashley and Alexandra—whom I love as my own. If I ever have children, these are the ones I want.

My friendship with Vanessa exceeds by just one day my friendship with her husband, and he collected me into his family like I was his sister. He even said that to me, soon after we met. He had a legal issue I was helping him with, and in the middle of our conversation he turned to me and said that if he had a sister he'd want her to be just like me. It was one of the nicest, most wonderful things anyone had ever said to me, and the way Vanessa and Tony brought me into their world was one of the nicest, most wonderful gifts. Think of it: For a friend to give you her family, as your family, is a rare and precious thing.

It's particularly wonderful that you *choose* to be a part of each other's lives. That's when you know you're in the company of a true friend. It's unconditional. It's without regret. There's no falsehood, no obligation. If something irritates you, you talk about it right then and move past it. You never second-guess the motives of your true friends. You don't even have to analyze their actions because you know, at bottom, that whatever they do or say or think flows in some fundamental way from the fact that they love you. It might come out wrong, but it all comes from the right place. I've never once gone to sleep wondering about something Vanessa said. Because I *know*. She's never hung up the phone after one of our late-night long-distance sessions and scratched her head over some fool thing that came out of my mouth. Because she *knows* too.

I imagine there was something of the same foundation between O. J. Simpson and Al Cowlings. There had to be, right? Probably O. J. didn't even have to ask A. C. to do anything extraordinary. Probably A. C. was just there, during his friend's most difficult time, and he found himself doing whatever needed to be done, whatever came naturally. I didn't know the first thing about these two men on the night of the Bronco chase, but I know enough now to know that A. C.'s actions came from a pure place in his heart. The only thing that mattered to him was that his friend was in trouble. Sometimes that's all you've got to go on, right? With good friends, it's almost like a marriage. For richer, for poorer. For better, for worse. In good times and bad. That's what a true friendship is really all about. You could almost exchange vows.

Later, when I had the chance to talk to A. C. about it, the first thing I told him was what a good friend he was. He didn't want to discuss the facts of the case. So we didn't discuss what he knew at the time or what he found out later. But I remember saying to him, "God, I hope I have a friend like you." And he said, "I hope you do too." He knew what he gave up, what he put at risk. He knew what it meant to put himself dead-smack in the middle of a big, fat, raging controversy, but I don't think it even occurred to him at the time. If he stopped to think about it, he would have seen he was in jeopardy. He would have seen the police, and the helicopters, and the media vans, and the sign-waving fanatics spilling out onto the highway. He would have known that when he pulled into the driveway on Rockingham, the Bronco would be in the sights of a hundred police weapons, and that when O. J. got ready to get out of the car with a gun in his hand all bets would be off. He would have put two and two together and come up with, "Oh, my God!" He would have processed what it all meant and considered his chances. But I can't imagine him thinking things through in just this way. Probably he didn't think things through at all. He was driven by his unconditional love for his friend, and willing to do whatever he needed to get him to the other side. Would O. J. have done the same thing for A. C.? That's between them. In some cases, the depths of friendship aren't quite reciprocal. In its purest form, friendship is about the pure place in two people's hearts that makes them gravitate toward each other and be willing to lay down their lives for each other. Then again, sometimes it's just about the pure place in one person's heart. But I'm lucky. I get to have a friend and be a friend, 'cause my friendship with Vanessa is mutual.

Friendship is a hard-to-figure thing. You can't always control it, or predict when it will turn up, or know where it will take you. You can't force it. When I first signed on to *The View,* that was one of my big worries. We all worried about it, Barbara Walters most of all. That's what the audition process was all about, for her. She even sent all of us who were up for the gig a little note, in which she basically said that her concept for the show wouldn't work unless the chemistry among her cohosts was real. Ours couldn't be a staged friendship, because the viewers would see right through that, but how the hell do you fabricate a relationship among a group of people who've never seen each other before in their lives? Who have nothing in common but the desire to land a good job alongside one of the great lights in broadcasting?

Naturally, we were all crazy-intimidated by the prospect of these manufactured friendships, but if that's what Barbara was looking for then that's what we'd try to give her. Hey, we all wanted the job, right? The producers ran a little focus-group test, to gauge the audience response to our interactions, and most of the people in the room thought Debbie and I had been friendly since forever. They thought Meredith and I had known each other professionally, because we complemented each other so well, and that none of us were intimidated by the presence of the great Barbara Walters. All of which was completely untrue. Debbie and I were about as unalike as two people could be. Meredith and I had never met. Everybody was intimidated. (Even Barbara, I think, was made a little bit anxious by the process.) But there was an unmistakable something going on during that audition. There was an immediate connection, and then when they took Barbara out of the mix and put Joy in her place, we continued to click.

By now, as we end our first season together, we've taken relationships that were indeed manufactured and turned them into something real. Our chemistry works on-screen because it works off-screen as well. It works in the office. It works when we go out to lunch or to do the town after the show. And it works when we call each other up on the phone at night—to dish, or to gab, or to talk seriously about whatever's going on in our lives that's commanding our attentions. We've become great friends, but if we're honest with ourselves we'll admit that these are still professional friendships. It might seem like an oxymoron—professional friendships?—but the friendship is key. Yes, we all get into our jeans and climb into our cars to drive out to Jersey to see Joy perform at one of her comedy clubs, but we do it because we want to, not because we have to. Joy's brilliantly funny, and dead-on. I'd go out to see her perform even if I didn't know her, but I consider myself lucky to call her a friend. (Of course, the downside to this is that she picks on us when she spots us in the audience; she rides me for being a diva; now, where does she get *that*?) But as much fun as we have together, as much as we've allowed ourselves to be drawn to each other, it still feels a little bit like we're trying each other on for size.

Remarkably, what Barbara has done is surrounded herself with four completely different people and willed us all into a tight little family. She's taken her magic wand and tapped us all on the shoulder and basically said, "Listen, and watch closely. This is how it's done." And never underestimate the power of Barbara Walters's magic wand, baby, because it's working. Even if people stopped watching us, and *The View* was canceled (which, of course, will never happen), we'd still have each other. No matter what happens to *The View*, or to our separate career paths, we'll always have each other. Just consider our differences. Debbie's this ridiculously attractive twenty-something person whose idea of a good night out is to go to Hogs and Heifers and dance on the bar and do shooters (even though I can drink her under the table); I may have been twenty-two once, but I was never *that* twenty-two. And yet, Debbie and I are remarkably close. I treat her like my baby sister. We even take some of our vacations together.

I love Meredith, and she says that I'm the sister she never had. We can finish each other's sentences. But she would rather be at home with her husband Richard and their three children than anyplace on this earth, so we can just forget about that vacation thing happening. Her integrity is unquestionable. She's a brilliant journalist who has won more Emmy awards than anyone I know. But she puts her family first. One of the things I admire most about her is that she refuses to compromise on raising children who will grow up knowing just how much they are loved. Nothing is more important.

Then there's my girl Joy—the Italian everyone in America thinks is Jewish thanks to her command of the Yiddish language. Joy adores her twenty-eight-year-old daughter, and her longtime boyfriend, Steve, whom we all call "Snuffy." Our experiences are nothing alike—

she spent her twenties and thirties raising her smart and very talented daughter, and didn't focus on her own career until much later on—and yet we've found our own common ground. And by the way, I'm glad she finally got around to developing her chops as a comedienne, because the world is a much funnier place with her in front of a microphone.

And Barbara's Barbara; she's one of the most celebrated women in the public eye (and deservedly so), and along the way she's broken every stereotype there is for a professional woman. I call her "B. W.," which makes her smile, but which also serves to remind her that even though she's the boss, we still consider her one of the girls. And she is.

So, clearly, these are not my contemporaries. We have nothing in common, really, other than the fact that we've grown on each other, and relied on each other, and gone through a tremendous personal and professional transformation in each other's midst. That said, I'd be blowing smoke if I claimed our friendships were as close as the one I share with someone like Vanessa, but we're on the right road. That's where we're headed. To get into that Bronco, you have to be willing to give up everything you are, everything you've learned, everything you want, and I don't give that away easily. No one should. And yet if I was sitting down to write this book a year from now, it wouldn't surprise me if we were all of us in the damn Bronco together, driving over some cliff. We'll be Thelma and Louise, squared. (Sort of.)

A good friendship takes time. It changes and evolves and matures, just as it does in a romantic relationship.

It's not something I have to work at, the way it sometimes feels I have to do with a guy, but it does take
time. The ones I love, I love. The ones I don't, I don't.
Now that I'm on it, though, I wonder if there isn't
some larger point to be made about the special friendships I share with my good girlfriends. What is it that
makes it easier for me to be myself, to completely
relax, around women? Why do I need my girlfriends,
and yet I'm content (for the time being, anyway) to do
without that one special man? Good questions all, and
I'm not sure I can answer them. I can try, though. In
my own head, at least, we women have got to look out
for each other, take care of each other, and set positive
examples for our little girls. Usually, women are the
harshest critics of women, and I see this as a good
thing, a necessary thing. In cases involving allegations of
rape or sexual harassment, for example, women are
much harder than men on the female accusers, and it's
probably because we put ourselves in the position of the
women involved and measure ourselves against their
actions. Or we measure them against us. We think, Oh,
well, I wouldn't have done the stupid stuff she did. Or,
I've been in that same situation and it wasn't such a big
deal. Or, You got what you deserved. We're much
harder. It's like female gynecologists are much rougher
than male gynecologists. Have you noticed this, or is it
just me? They know that whatever they've got to do is
gonna hurt for a second, but it's not gonna kill you, so
they just go and get it over with. The men are so much
gentler because they don't know; they've studied the
female body, but they don't have the same parts, so
they don't know.

We see the same thing, in reverse, in the White House sex scandals occupying a little bit much of our media attention at the time of this writing. Men are harder on President Clinton than women are, and I think the reason is because they all know what dirty dogs men can be, and they're pissed at him for making such a public spectacle of the fact. They can think, I'd never let my dirty laundry hang out to dry like that, and they string him up for giving a bad name to the rest of the species. Women are much more forgiving of the president, because we know that even in this day and age sometimes you've got to look the other way when it comes to a man's ability to keep it in his pants.

We women rely on each other, absolutely. Because sometimes, you know, men let you down. Life happens, but in the middle of it and underneath and all around, women allow themselves to be much more emotionally attached to their friends than men do. We get involved in each other's lives. We're involved with each other's children. We're in each other's heads. We help each other pick out our underwear and clothing. Men don't do that.

All of which makes Al Cowlings's actions on that memorable evening all the more remarkable. It just wasn't a *guy* thing to do. Yeah, men have always watched each other's backs, and stood up for each other. (The whole notion of having a "second" at a fight is a real guy thing, if you ask me.) But until A. C., that kind of behavior seemed rooted in a ritualistic code. With the Bronco ride, though, it was all reaction. That's how I saw it, as this pure, visceral thing, no questions asked, no matter what, come what may. It was a friend in trouble and a friend at the ready, and as I've reflected on that night in the years since, I've often wondered where I'd be, what I'd do, how I'd react to a similar set of circumstances. Of course, I can't know, but I can wonder, and I can see it for what it is: the mark of a true friend.

Now, hand me the keys, Vanessa. And I'll be sure to let you know when I need a ride.

Be Careful What You
Pray For

❧

I am the modern, intelligent, independent-type woman—
in other words, a girl who cannot get a man.
— SHELLEY WINTERS

I DON'T LIKE short guys. I'm sorry, but I never
have. I don't care if you're overweight or underweight,
but you should at least have some height to you. You
should at least be as tall as me in four-inch heels.

The man I marry needs to be smart. Bill Gates
smart. Michael Eisner smart. And passionate. Bodice-
ripper passionate. Michael Douglas in *Basic Instinct* passionate. He needs to be handsome. I'm not insisting on
drop-dead, Denzel Washington gorgeous; just plain
handsome is okay.

Attractive. I don't want anybody spending more time in the mirror than I do, or more time looking at their own reflections than they do looking at mine; a handsome man who cares just the right amount about his appearance is what I'm after. He should have a sense of style too. Torn jeans and T-shirts are fine for around the house, but he's got to style when we're on the town. He's got to make me look good.

What else? Let's see. . . . He needs to be fun-loving, adventuresome. I don't mean he has to be out there snowboarding or skydiving—because, Lord knows, I'm not gonna join him—but he should be open to new things. He should be able to teach me something, and willing to let me teach him. He should have a good relationship with his family—or, at least, a good reason for not having a good relationship with his family. He should have a good heart, and a place in his life for God. I want a man who feels good about himself, but I can't see spending the rest of my life with a man who thinks he can master his own universe, without the help of God.

I haven't limited myself to dating only black men. I don't choose my friends based on their skin color, so I'm certainly not going to choose a mate that way. I want a man who is kind and gentle and treats me like I hung the moon. If that man happens to be African-American, Latin, Asian, Caucasian, Native American, or otherwise, I'm going to return his call. Don't get me wrong: If I had to state a preference, I'd want a strong black man like my father and grandfathers. Like Vanessa's husband Tony, or his father Fred. Like my friend and "brother" Samuel L. Jackson, and the scores of other men who have come into my life. It's just that I decided a long time ago to play with all the crayons in the box, and not limit myself based on what others would have me do. Time out for that.

Lately, one of my main considerations is that the guy has got to be fairly user-friendly and maintenance-free. I expect to have to deal with *some* baggage when it comes to hooking up with a new guy (God knows, I have a fully matched set), but it has to be carry-on. Know what I mean? If I'm gonna put myself out there for another person, it can't be so much work that I'm unable to see some kind of payoff. If there's work to be done later on, after we're committed to each other, then that's another matter, but going in, with all the choices I've got these days, I'm not looking to make an extra effort. Sue me, but I'm just not.

Now, I know this little checklist I've set out puts me across with more than a little arrogance of my own, but that's just how it is, baby. If you've read with me this far, and if you've listened to me on television, you'll know I don't put up with a lot of unnecessary nonsense, so why should I be any different in my personal life? There's necessary nonsense in every relationship, right? All I'm doing is looking to cut back on the unnecessary stuff. Who's got time for that? I certainly don't.

If you want to know the truth, I work hard at my relationships. I shouldn't have to, but I do. Friendships come easy to me, as I've written; it's the romantic relationships that take some doing. I put a lot of emphasis on the small things, and maybe not enough on some of the big things. I worry over what I wear and what I say, and in the back of my head, at the beginning of every relationship, there's a little voice reminding me, "A date is not necessarily a mate." Just because you go out with someone, just because you maybe even spend the night with someone or go away for the weekend, it doesn't mean you should start picking out china patterns. But I've been guilty of that before, and I'll be guilty of that again, I'm sure.

It's been my experience that men don't usually have this problem. (Here I go with my sweeping generalities again, but what the hell . . . it's my book.) They're genetically programmed not to think long-term. Even when they ask you to marry 'em, they're not thinking long-term. Yet. They'll walk down the aisle and *then* start to think, Oh, damn, I'm about to do this thing. My male friends tell me this happens all the time, but we women often walk down that aisle in our heads before we sit down to our first meal together, for goodness' sake. We think things all the way through, before there's anything to think about beyond a nice-enough date with a nice-enough guy.

Where I differ from most women is in my definition of long-term. For a whole lot of my girlfriends, it's Marry me or move on, and that attitude spills forth at every opportunity. A woman will start a conversation with, "Would you like our children to go to private school or public school?" Right? And the man will look at her like she just turned into a lizard, because it's only their third date. I have done this. I have invited a man over for dinner on a third date and turned our conversation down the same path. We had our first date, at some fancy restaurant. We had our movie date. And there I was, cooking him dinner, having a glass of champagne, and slipping, "So, if I were to have your child, would you want it to be a boy or a girl?" into the conversation.

What the hell was I thinking? And forget me. What the hell was he thinking? There was nothing in the world the guy could say, except to stammer some Jackie Gleason/Ralph Kramden impression—"Ubbidi, ubbida, ubbidi, ubbida . . ."—and look frantically for the door.

Even if he'd indulged me a bit and gotten into the conversation, his heart would have been someplace else, and his head would have been wondering, What's up with her? How do I get out of this? I extrapolated a completely ridiculous premise and put it out there for him to consider, and then I built whole other ridiculous premises off of how he appeared to be considering it. "Oh, he really does like me if he's talking about having children with me." Or, "Oh, this isn't happening, because he doesn't want to talk about having children with me." Really, all I should have been worrying about was dinner, and making sure his champagne glass was full, and seeing if this third date might lead to a fourth, but there was a little too much going on in my head for that. A little too much and not nearly enough, all at the same time.

I've been working to change this type of behavior, with some success. Lately, I tell myself I enjoy going out, I enjoy dating, I enjoy having great conversations with men, and then I leave it at that. I recognize it's a date, and if it's someone I'm really interested in I'll find a way to let him know without scaring him off. This way it's straight, and open. It took me a while to get to this point, and I still have a ways to go, but it's a much healthier approach, don't you think?

Like I said, my idea of a long-term relationship doesn't quite measure up to those of most of the women I know. The longest I've been with a guy has been about two years, and that was with Leo. Leonardo Alejandro Arturo Felipe Luis Berrojo, the sexiest, sweetest, kindest, most gorgeous man you'll ever meet. Leo was born in Florida, but his family comes from the Dominican Republic. He and I hooked up in Los Angeles, on the set of *Jones & Jury,* my venture into the uncertain world of syndicated television. The premise of *Jones & Jury* was sort of like *People's Court* for the nineties, with me as the host judge and the audience acting like the jury who would decide a small-claims case. Anyway, we did the show in front of a studio audience, and the premise was that we'd pick one person out of the crowd to stand as the foreman of the jury. The entire audience would render its verdict on whatever case we were exploring that day, and the foreman would serve as a kind of spokesperson.

One day, we were having some technical difficulties, and I started what I thought was a whispered conversation with my executive producer, Howard Schultz, during one of the breaks. I had a little microphone, which I assumed—incorrectly—was connected only to the control booth, and I was just talking back and forth to Howard while the technicians were troubleshooting the problem. "Who's the foreman today?" I asked, thinking no one could hear me but Howard.

"See that guy up there?" he said, back into my ear. I could see him pointing. "That tall, good-looking one?"

I waved to the tall, good-looking guy in the audience—Leo—and he waved back. Then I whispered into my microphone and said, "You finally find a cute one for me, and he's married." I could see, from my place on the stage, a gold band on the ring finger of the foreman's left hand.

But guess what? This idle comment, intended for Howard's ears, had been broadcast to the entire studio. The audience burst out laughing, and Leo blushed, and I was mortified. Then Leo stood. "No, I'm not," he shouted across the studio, holding up his hand and indicating his ring. "It's not a wedding ring," he explained.

With this, the audience went, "Woooooooooo," as studio audiences have a tendency to do in the land of daytime television.

Howard Schultz wasn't one to let such an opening go unnoticed, especially when he had some time to fill and a good thing going. "So," he said to Leo over the microphone, "Miss Jones thinks you're a good-looking guy. What do you think of Miss Jones?"

"Miss Jones is a beautiful woman," Leo replied, very much on the spot, and before either one of us knew what happened Howard had thrown a couple more logs on the fire and tried to heat things up between us. It was all silly, and merely meant as a harmless diversion, but once we got past our technical difficulties I couldn't stop thinking about it. All through the taping, I kept thinking, That's the cutest guy I'll ever see. I hope he comes up to talk to me after the show. What am I gonna say? Would I really go out with a member of my studio audience? He could be a lunatic. About a million scenarios were lining up for my attention. Imagine: me, a grown woman, a grown professional woman, a former prosecuting attorney now with her own television show, lost in such schoolgirl musings in front of 150 strangers.

At the end of the show, I flagged down one of our production assistants and asked her to get this guy's number. To this day, I don't know what possessed me to do this. I guess I just figured, Why not? She came back a few minutes later and said, "You'll never believe what he said. He said he was wondering if he should come backstage and leave his phone number. He said he was hoping he'd find a way to meet you." I'm telling you, it was like high school all over again. Really, it was a little embarrassing, and now that I think back on it, this poor little production assistant must have felt like a pimp, the way I cast her as a go-between. The rest of the crew soon sniffed what was going on, and everyone started teasing me mercilessly, but I just tucked away Leo's card with his phone number on it and put it in a safe place. Later, when I flipped it over, I saw he'd written something on the back: "Would love to get together."

That night, in the car on the way home, I called him. I just thought to myself, Star, go for it. I kept coming back to how adorable this guy was, and I just couldn't let this opening close, even if it was against my better judgment. Besides, my better judgments are rarely more suitable than my regular ones, so I simply set this one aside and made the call. He wasn't in, so I left a message on his answering machine. A part of me was relieved not to have to talk to him directly—what would I have said?—but another part froze at the thought that I might leave the wrong kind of message. Don't you just hate that long moment before the beep, when you have to think what to say? It's one of life's pressure-packed social situations. As I waited for Leo's beep I thought to myself, Whatever you do, don't sound desperate. Don't sound too full of yourself or too smitten with him. At the beep, I thanked him for playing along with us in the studio, and apologized for putting him in an awkward position, and told him I owed him a beer next time he came by. I hung up thinking I'd struck just the right tone, and left the next move up to him. Either he would call, or he wouldn't. I'd stuck my neck through that opening without climbing all the way through. (A girl has to preserve her dignity, don't you think?)

Well, the very next day, Leo came to the studio to collect on his beer, but I invited him instead to have dinner backstage. We were taping three shows that day, with a dinner break stuck somewhere in the middle, and I thought it might be a good way to break the ice. You know, there were people around, we wouldn't worry what to wear, I'd have to get back to work in just a little bit. It seemed a pretty stress-free way to get a first date under our belts, and Leo apparently agreed. He said he thought dinner sounded great. The rest of the staff was a little weirded out by the idea at first, because, after all, we had a lot of kooks and loonies in our studio audience—some of them people pulled right off the street, or from some shopping mall, just to fill seats. This guy could have been a mad rapist, for all anyone knew.

But Leo was wonderful. He wanted to be an actor. He had no money. He was, it turned out, almost ten years younger than me, which struck me initially as kinda cool. I'd never dated someone so young, and yet he didn't feel young to me. In fact, everything about him seemed exactly right: his look, his demeanor, his disposition. And goodness, he was gorgeous! Maybe this was the guy I was looking for. At some point, at around the time I had to go back to work, I pointed to his left hand and said, "I can't believe that dumb ring brought us together."

"This?" he said, slipping it off his finger. "I bought it down on Melrose for, like, seven bucks." He handed it to me. "I want you to have it," he said. "Something to remember me by."

I took it and put it on my finger, this cheap little ring, right between a gorgeous diamond engagement ring, left to me by my great-aunt, and a stunning diamond cluster ring I'd bought as an indulge-myself present soon after I collected my first big-time television paycheck. These were my good-luck pieces of jewelry, and Leo's cheap ring fit right in. I put it on without even thinking about it, and when the time came for me to go back in to makeup, to prepare for the next show, it was clear to both of us we wanted to get together again. And soon.

"I owe you a beer," I finally said, thinking that as long as I came into this thing all bold and forward I might as well see it through. "How 'bout we meet for a drink after the show?"

Leo picked the place—a wild bar in downtown Hollywood. I went to meet him after our last show, and it was completely over the top. The place was filled with a wild young Hollywood crowd—gays, straights, transvestites. You name it, this was their place. We started laughing and talking and dancing. No question, we were flirting, and before long Leo and I were doing body shots. I'd like to report that I had never heard of body shots, but to tell the truth they were my idea. Remember, I was in flirt mode. With body shots, what you do is put lemon on your bare shoulder, and salt, and then your date licks the salt off your skin, with the lemon, and drinks a shot of tequila. You lick his shoulder and he licks yours. They're more like mating shots, really, and by the end of the evening, needless to say, they worked.

We were together for the next year and a half, and it was so wonderful, so much fun. We traveled to Europe together. We did the Hollywood scene together. We lived up in the hills, in a beautiful leased home. Ultimately, I think it was this lavish lifestyle that got in the way of our relationship. Most struggling actors don't live this way, and Leo started to feel a little strange about it after a while. I started to feel a little strange too, on Leo's behalf. I had a very good income, now that I had my own television show, and I chose to spend it on myself in certain ways, and on Leo in certain ways, by extension. My lifestyle was okay with Leo for the time being, but it started to gnaw at him when he looked ahead to our future. After a year together, you start to think long-term. You do. It's What are we doing here? Is this relationship going anywhere? Should we get married? These are the kinds of questions you ask yourself, and each other. I was in my thirties; he was in his twenties. My friends used to tease and call him my boy toy, and his friends used to tease and call me his sugar mama. We knew what we were to each other, and this gap in our ages and our incomes was not what broke us up. What broke us up, I think, was that Leo needed to become the man we both knew he could be, and I needed to stretch. What we had was a fun relationship, but there was no future in it at just that time, and we were both mature enough and honest enough to recognize this and move on.

The best part of our relationship is that it continues to this day. Leo still occasionally acts, but really has become quite the accomplished producer and supervises several television shows. Our friendship is deeper than before, and we still find time for an occasional intimate moment. That's been the key, our relationship was grounded in friendship, so when the intimacy ended the friendship remained. Still, it doesn't stop us from those pangs of jealousy when we hear about each other's new loves. The bond is still there, and neither one of us knows what will ultimately happen between us. For now, Leo has pledged that if I'm still unmarried and without children at forty, he'll do the deed. It's a sweet gesture, but I'm not exactly counting on it, if you know what I mean.

See, I'm one of those people who believe a relationship is part of the package. It's not the whole package, and when I become involved with someone I look to fit that person into my already established life. You don't try to fit your life into the relationship. At least, I don't

—especially this deep into my adulthood. If you try to make that relationship your entire life, you're gonna be in trouble if something goes wrong. That's why women whose lives revolve around their husband's business, whose friends are only those people she's met through their shared social circle, wake up one morning with a look of sheer shock when they realize their marriages are over and the rest of their lives are empty.

My theory is you've always got to have Plan B. If Plan A doesn't work out, you've got to have another option. Don't misunderstand me: I hope and dream of a Cinderella ending to every new relationship. Plan A —the fairy tale plan—is always the preferred plan. But I always have a contingency plan in my head. What do you do if he turns out to be a frog? For this reason, I always have an internal prenup bouncing around in my head. It's who I am, and how I go about the stuff of my life. I approached law school the same way. You want things to work out for the best, but you have to prepare for the worst.

Of course, it's always gonna hurt when things sour, no matter how you prepared for the souring. Damn right, it hurts, but at least you can see your way through to the other side. You're madly in love, and he's perfect, and he's the beginning and the end and the alpha and the omega and all is well and you're just so completely smitten and besotted and committed, and he turns to you one day and says, "Here's my platinum American Express card. Go to Saks. Buy yourself something sexy. I'm taking you to Bali next week." So you go to Saks, and you buy yourself something sexy, and you're bubbling over with happiness, and you're feeling so great you decide to bounce over to his house just to give him a hug, and you show up and find him with some Becky, already there. What do you do now? What the hell do you do now?

You've got to know where the exit is, girl. You've got to have a next move up your sleeve. You can hope like hell to never have to use it, but you've got to think in terms of worst-case scenarios. You've got to have Plan B.

Look, I'm a sucker for romance, but I won't be a sucker for some guy. I love it, in the movies, when the guy gets the girl and the girl gets the guy. But if I were Debra Winger in *An Officer and a Gentleman*, and Richard Gere came into my factory to sweep me off my feet and carry me into the happily-ever-after, I'd be thinking, What's next? I'd be thinking, I hope this works out, but if it doesn't I want to make sure I can come back to this job in the factory. Just in case. I fully believe this makes me a stronger, better-balanced person than someone who simply throws her hands up in the air and says, "Whatever will be, will be." That was the mantra of so many women, back when Doris Day used to sing "Que Será, Será," but that message doesn't cut it anymore. I don't know that it ever did.

And so, just in case, I'm thinking of having my eggs frozen. I'm not ready for a family just yet, but someday I might be, and when that day comes there may not be a Mr. Right in the picture. I'm a Girl Scout gone a little bit berserk: I'm always prepared for every eventuality. Just in case.

There have been some wonderful men in my life,

but I'm still waiting for that unconditional, say-what-you-think,   it's-okay-to-trust-you-for-the-rest-of-my-life kind of wonderful. I see what my mother and father have, what my mother's parents have, what Donald's parents had, and I know it hasn't found me yet. It will, I'm sure of it, but I'm still waiting. I've had fun, I've been madly in love, and I can remember a time when my heart just sang. But for some reason, the song's always ended.

Still, I know there's something else out there. I know how I feel about my friends, and I know I should feel at least as good about the man who's mine. I trust that. I go to sleep at night secure in the fact that one day my heart will sing an aria. I don't deserve anything less.

Trumping the Race Card

❦

If Western civilization does not now respond
constructively to the challenge to banish racism, some
future historian will have to say that a great civilization
died because it lacked the soul and commitment
to make justice a reality for all men.
—MARTIN LUTHER KING, JR.

THE FIRST TIME I started to really formulate who
I was as a lawyer came in the trial of a bad guy named
James Miller, who was accused of kidnapping two
young girls in Brooklyn Heights in May 1988. It was
also the first time I started to think about the ways we
on the side of the law sometimes abuse our positions
for something less than the public interest.

James Miller was a black man in his late thirties, a
known pedophile and a convicted sex offender who had
been released from prison less than a month earlier

after serving fourteen years for the double rape of two children in the same neighborhood. This information, naturally, was kept from the jury, on the fair-minded theory that if the jurors knew this man's record they'd convict him before sorting through the facts of the case. I understood this, even if I had to bite my tongue in court to keep from blurting out the truth of this man's nature; it's sometimes tough to play by the rules when the rules make sense and still seem designed to keep you from your goal. It fell to me, then, to convince the jury that James Miller was indeed as despicable as we all knew him to be, and that he deserved to be punished for his actions on this one day.

On this one day, not even three weeks into his new freedom, Miller made the mistake of grabbing a four-teen-year-old Hispanic girl wheeling an eighteen-month-old Caucasian baby in a stroller. He put a knife to the older child's throat and forced her to wheel the baby into an open vestibule. It was a high-profile case, chiefly because of the contemptible nature of Miller's crime, but also because the baby's parents were a prominent television news correspondent and a noted screenwriter. The teenage girl was the daughter of the baby's regular nanny, and she was taking the child for a walk along the promenade, down by the water, some-thing she'd done a dozen times before. It was a beauti-ful day, in the kind of nice, safe neighborhood where bad things don't usually happen, and this was another reason the case made headlines; it seemed to strike a certain segment of New Yorkers just a little too close to home.

The Brooklyn waterfront was crowded with well-dressed people enjoying a delightful afternoon—couples, mothers and their children, other baby-sitters with their young charges. The teenager stopped and helped the baby smell some flowers, and at this point Miller sneaked up behind the older girl, grabbed her around the neck, and put a knife to her throat in such a way that no one else could see the weapon. "Walk," he said. And she did.

At this point, in what I said in court was a fluke of God looking out for these children, two other teenagers ditching school, Annette Gálvez and David Goodwin, happened to notice what was going on and decided to follow Miller on their bicycles. Visualize this with me: a black man, with his arm around the neck of a Hispanic girl, who in turn was pushing a white, blond, blue-eyed baby in a stroller. Clearly, something was wrong with this picture, and to top it off the older child had tears streaming down her face. The entire scene seemed "off" to these other kids, and they started playing Nancy Drew. (Actually, since it was a guy and a girl—boyfriend and girlfriend—it was more like Nancy Drew and one of the Hardy boys.) They followed Miller and the two girls they figured for his victims along the promenade, and then through the neighborhood. They didn't have a plan, but they were determined to keep an eye on things; only when Miller started jimmying the doorknobs of the buildings along the street they figured they needed a more proactive approach. One of the kids went to find a police officer, while the other stayed back and kept an eye on Miller, who was frantically trying to find an open doorway and still keep the older girl from screaming.

Into this scene came Police Officer Daniel Ingoldsby —a big, wonderful man who responded beautifully to the call. Instead of just telling the teenager on the bicycle to move along, like too many cops would have done, he got on it immediately. The scenario must have seemed pretty far-fetched, but he followed the bicyclist back to the scene on foot, and he arrived in time to see the bad guy fleeing. Eventually, James Miller had figured out he was being followed, and he let the kids go, but not before threatening the fourteen-year-old. "If you tell anyone about this," he said, "I'll kill you. I'll kill your family. I know where you live and how to find you." Of course, he didn't know any such thing, but this is the way you scare an already frightened little girl into keeping quiet.

Ingoldsby gave chase, and David Goodwin took after Miller on his bike as well, while Annette Gálvez went to comfort the two children. After a couple blocks, they ran Miller down, and Ingoldsby arrested him, and at first it seemed like a sigh-of-relief ending to what could have been a terrible tragedy. No one was hurt, they got the bad guy, there were corroborating eyewitness accounts, and it was an open-and-shut case, right? Well, not quite. Indeed, by the time the case came to me it had already been tried once, ending in a hung jury. Another assistant district attorney, John Ross, caught the case the first time around, and he was confronted with a defense that in later years would come to be known as the "race card" defense. Back then, it was just a desperate, unnamed strategy; when the facts didn't support your case, you used race to your advantage if you were of a different race than the people accusing you. I should mention here that I bristle whenever the issue of race is dismissed as a "card" to be played. It diminishes the issue. If racism applies, there are no cards involved. There are no games. There are real issues to be confronted. If it's just being used as an excuse or a diversion, then it's just bullshit, and it was bullshit here.

In the first trial, defense attorney Joe Giannini somehow managed to convince the jury that James Miller was being persecuted, not prosecuted, because he was a black man who dared to walk around in a white neighborhood. Ingoldsby, the police officer, never actually saw the defendant with the two children; he only saw him running down the street, and the defense attorney maintained that though Miller was indeed running he wasn't necessarily fleeing. He had no reason to flee. He was just moving on and going about his business. Giannini very neatly turned it into a credibility argument, one side versus the other—the teenagers who'd been ditching school against a black man whose only crime was being a black man who looked suspicious.

Remember, the jurors couldn't know about Miller's prior convictions, so all they had to go on were the facts of the case and the testimony offered in court. The fourteen-year-old girl was on hand to tell her side of the story, but Giannini was able to defuse her testimony by reminding the jury that she was young, and terrified, and really unable to see her attacker because she had been approached from behind. The testimony of the two bicyclists was somewhat discounted because they had been skipping out of school at the time of the incident (and were, therefore, unreliable), and because they too had only seen the attacker from behind. The police officer, for his part, could only report that he had seen the defendant running down the street.

In New York, a hung jury meant we could try the case again, within the time the statute provided for a speedy trial, and I was called in to Elizabeth Holtzman's office and given the case. Holtzman, the Brooklyn DA at the time, and a onetime candidate for United States senator and for New York City mayor, was in some ways playing her own version of the race card, and here it was a purely defensive move. I was one of a handful of black females in the felony bureaus able to try this kind of case, and among them I was probably the loudest, with a recent string of very public successes to my credit. It was the first time I'd been summoned to the boss's office and given a case, and to tell you the truth I was a little surprised by the call. I wasn't a part of the ''sex crimes'' unit, so I had never tried a sexual assault case; even though Miller hadn't done anything of a sexual nature we all knew what he had in mind for these girls.

Up until this time, I'd only been vaguely familiar with the details surrounding the case, and Holtzman brought me up to speed. She told me what John Ross had come up against in court, and what she was hoping to get from me. She told me that as long as the defense attorney was choosing to make this case about race, it wouldn't hurt to have a black prosecutor; if she could find a black woman for the job, then so much the better.

The charge against Miller was kidnapping—a B felony, which would carry up to a twenty-five-year prison sentence if we managed to convict. What I needed, I told my boss, was to meet the family of the baby girl, and the baby-sitter's family. If I couldn't get that teenager to trust me, we wouldn't have a case, so I sat down with both families and went to work. Here, I think, I began to develop a reputation in the district attorney's office regarding the manner in which I'd approach a case. I would go the extra yard, and take the time, and do whatever it took to prepare. I wanted her to feel like I was going to protect her on the witness stand, because I knew her testimony would be the key to our case. If she wasn't comfortable up there, Giannini would have this second jury doubting her credibility all over again.

Now, this case followed by several years the case of the rap singer accused of stabbing his ex-girlfriend's new boyfriend. In that one, you'll recall, I was all over myself for blurring the lines between a personal and a professional relationship with my witnesses. This time, though, I didn't set out to inflate my own sense of self-worth. I wasn't looking to make friends, or looking at myself through the eyes of my witnesses. This time it was a trial strategy versus an ego-stroking expedition for a young prosecuting attorney. A key distinction. I'd learned my lesson, but I also knew that this little girl and I had to connect on a personal level or we'd get nowhere. We went over the case. She told me what her dreams were about school; I told her what I was hoping to get out of life. I got the feeling no one ever talked to this girl as an adult, and it appeared to do wonderful things for her self-esteem. The closer we got to the trial, the less I worried about her ability to come across on the stand as competent and credible. Naturally, I didn't give her the words to tell what happened, but I helped her to find the confidence and courage she needed to be an effective witness.

Joe Giannini was the nemesis of many of my colleagues, and with this case he became mine. He'd beaten pretty much everybody in my office, several times, and most of us couldn't stand him. He was a short, cocky Italian lawyer who thought he was just a little bit more entitled to walk this earth than anyone else, and I suppose he looked across the aisle at me and thought I carried myself the same way. It all comes down to perspective, doesn't it? He was trying to do his job, and I was trying to do mine, and as long as we did our jobs well we would always be at cross-purposes.

The trial itself went pretty much as I anticipated. Giannini played the so-called race card again, and my witness was very sure of herself and very strong. It came down to a question of credibility—my witness versus James Miller, who although he didn't testify sat there cloaked in the presumption of innocence. He was a man with a record of prior convictions that would have surely sent him away for another twenty years, if the jury had only known. But, of course, the jurors couldn't know, and I cringed when Giannini went into his summation. I knew what he would say—that Miller was falsely accused, a black man in the wrong place at the wrong time—but I was outraged just the same. I knew what the defendant had done, what he was capable of, what he might do again if we let him back out on the street. And so, when I stood to offer my own summation, I let my anger show a little bit. I knew I could win the jurors back to my side of what happened, if I could somehow demonstrate the full flavor of my indignation.

The jurors were mostly middle-class, mostly black. It was my kind of jury. Why? Because middle-class blacks are the people whose lives are most touched by violent crime. Their televisions are getting stolen; they're the ones getting robbed at the ATM; it's their children who are coopted by gangs, or seduced by drugs. Their neighborhoods are in peril. These are the folks who would love to see justice served, but they always held me to my burden of proof. They'd stare back at me as if to say, "You either got it or you don't, Miss Jones."

In this case, I had it, and I wasn't about to let James Miller walk on the back of some misguided notions of prejudice. No way. I stood before those jurors and told them I was outraged, personally and professionally, at Giannini's decision to make race an issue in this trial. This didn't have anything to do with this man's color. He didn't get arrested because he was black. He got arrested because he grabbed these children, and put a knife to the older girl's throat, and took off with them down the street. "Society" didn't conspire to make James Miller do these things, and "society" didn't serve him up to pay for someone else's crime. It was all on him.

You know, outside the courtroom, with some distance, I don't blame Joe Giannini for trying. If that was all he had, he was obligated to use it. I wasn't mad at him, but I did want to convey to the jury that what he had was crap. Years later, during the O. J. Simpson trial, folks were all over Johnnie Cochran for playing what they thought was the race card the way he did, but I understood it for what it was. It may have been reaching, but at least it was built around the evidence he had. Cochran played every card available to him, and that's the defense attorney's job. You've got to play the hand. You'd never take the ace of spades out of your hand in a game of poker. That would be dumb. Cochran wasn't dumb. Giannini wasn't dumb. I had no problem with his trying whatever defense he thought was available to him.

What I had a problem with was that it had worked when there was no evidence of racism at all, and that it might work again, so I made it my business to see that it didn't. I told the jury that Giannini's line was about the biggest package of bull they'd ever been handed, and in the end I was persuasive enough in my summation, and Officer Ingoldsby and the little girl and the two bicyclists were persuasive enough in their testimonies, that the jury was able to see through the smoke of Giannini's argument and come back with a conviction.

Here's where I made it personal. All through the trial, James Miller was flashing me stares of such intense hatred that I couldn't look away. He fixed on me with more venom than I'd ever encountered from a defendant. Understand, this man was a convicted sex offender—a pervert, a child rapist who took his pleasure in hurting little kids. He couldn't touch me, but his obvious hatred was still a bit frightening. I wanted him to pay all over again for what he'd done in the past, for what he tried to do to these two children, but more than that I wanted to crucify him, and when we moved from conviction to sentencing I pulled out the heavy artillery. Here, at last, I could introduce this man's record into the proceedings, and the way I did it was perhaps my most manipulative act as a prosecutor. It was a brilliant move, if I say so myself. I'd gone back through Miller's record and uncovered two juvenile offenses—a rape and a robbery—dating back before the statutes had changed to where you couldn't use juvenile records in an adult sentencing. In New York, if you commit three violent felonies within a determined stretch of time, you can be sentenced as if you committed murder—even if one of those felonies was committed as a minor. So I argued that Miller's time spent in prison didn't count against the statute of limitations in this case, and moved to have him sentenced as a predicate felon offender, which carried a sentence of twenty-five years to life.

Well, if James Miller had been looking at me with hatred up until this point, he now looked at me as if his eyes would burst from their sockets. Really, I thought his head would explode. Giannini's too. No one had been expecting this—not even the judge, who leaned back in his chair and offered what I took to be a smile, as if to say, "Not bad." He knew what this man had done, and I imagine he wanted to see him put away as much as I did. And, indeed, he did. The judge handed down the maximum—twenty-five to life—and Miller was apoplectic. He'd gone from a hung jury and having what he must have thought was a reasonable shot at beating this thing, to most likely spending the rest of his life behind bars. And he blamed me for the change in his fortunes. Not himself. Me. Truly, he was the nastiest, most out-of-control defendant I'd ever gone up against in court. I'd gone for the jugular, and then I took out a knife and slit this pervert's throat. That's really what I did, and I admit it. And yet it was all within the law—and all within the confines of what this guy deserved. He had it coming.

He also had my movie line coming, which I'd been saving for just this moment. It had been in my arsenal since I began practicing law, and James Miller walked right into it. He screamed at me from across the courtroom, "I'll get you, you bitch! No matter where you are, no matter how long it takes. You'll never know a minute's peace, because I will get you, you bitch." The man was running out of material—it was pretty much the same threat he'd issued to my fourteen-year-old victim—but I had a ready response.

"Mr. Miller," I shouted back, with all the confidence of a full-of-herself twenty-six-year-old who'd just done the right thing. "I'd be afraid, but for the fact that your parole officer hasn't even been born yet."

It was a great line, and I'd been itching to use it ever since I'd seen it in some movie years earlier, and now that it was delivered and out there I felt a tremendous rush of satisfaction. It was manipulative, absolutely, but it felt great, even if it was more than a little melodramatic. Still, I don't think I ever experienced a deeper sense of accomplishment than I had in watching them lock James Miller's perverted ass up, and seeing this look wash over his face as he realized he was gone. That's when I knew I was doing the right thing.

That case taught me a great deal—to pick and choose my moments, to let the other guy play his best hand but be sure to beat him with yours, to give the letter of the law some room to find its mark. Most times, in the hands of the right prosecutor, justice will prevail, despite the smoke and mirrors of some of our most celebrated defense attorneys. Like I said, the so-called race card is just one of the cards in the deck available to defense attorneys and prosecuting attorneys, as long as it's played ethically and legally. Yeah, it irritates me, and it makes me want to throw a plate at somebody, but then I look around at the world we live in and realize it is sometimes a fair thing, to charge that someone has been arrested, convicted, sentenced, or targeted simply because they're black, Hispanic, Latin, Asian, what have you. That happens. It happens in this country every day. Race *can* be an issue, and it often is, but it should never be an excuse. Race is not an excuse. Age is not an excuse. Gender is not an excuse. The circumstances of your birth are just that—circumstances. So it's up to you to make those circumstances work for you.

About a year after this, in a case that wasn't mine but felt like it was, Giannini used the same tactic. This time it was in the trial for the murder of a police officer I had worked with and befriended. The officer, Robert Machate Jr. was a bit of a "cowboy" in that he did things his way, as some cops on the street often do. He was good at his job, and together, he and his partner, Gus Cecchini, piled up "collars" and acted like they were the princes of the city. In March 1989, Machate and Cecchini came up against a creep named Reynaldo Rayside and one of his compatriots during a routine traffic stop. Something went terribly wrong and

Machate was killed. He left a wife, an unborn child, a family who loved him, and friends who would miss him terribly. The city mourned.

As you might imagine, the murder of a police officer always sends our law enforcement efforts into overdrive. The cops caught the alleged perpetrators right near the scene, within hours of the ambush, and the case looked fairly open-and-shut. But it wasn't. Machate was white and Rayside was black, and Brooklyn was always a powder keg whenever race was a factor. Giannini made it a factor: He poked holes in Cecchini's recollections; he introduced the theory of white cops targeting blacks on the street; he even floated the idea that Machate had died from the friendly fire of his white partner, who now blamed a black man in a cover-up. He caused doubt in such a way it made my stomach turn. And it worked. Rayside was acquitted of the more serious charge of murder, and convicted of a lesser charge. Such a thing was virtually unheard of! The murder of a police officer, going unpunished? I thought the world had opened up and gone mad. I wanted to shout out in court that Rayside's race didn't matter. As far as I was concerned, the prosecution had presented ample evidence that Rayside was a cold-blooded murderer who had killed a good man, and that was where it should have ended.

In some ways, this case marked the beginning of the end for me in the district attorney's office. Granted, this wasn't my case, but if a jury couldn't see through this obvious charade, how could I possibly keep doing what I was doing? What was especially galling was that the prosecution failed to confront the race card dealt by the defense. We could have put this guy away if the individual prosecutors were able to speak honestly about the racial issue. We could have trumped the race card and thrown it back at the defense, but some people are just too afraid to discuss race in completely open terms. Among whites, there's this fear that they will be called racist if they misspeak or use a wrong phrase. Among blacks, there's a perception that you're selling out if you fail to side with one of your own. Racism scares me, because it wakes me up. Sometimes I get complacent in my little world of success and privilege and forget that even though this is the late 1990s, some people will look at me and fail to see the smart, successful African-American woman who sits before them. Some people will look at me and simply see a nigger. Things have changed in our country, but not so much that there are no more battles to fight and no more fights to win. So you see, I know that racism is alive and well and living in America. Just quit trying to trade on that fact in a court of law as an excuse for inappropriate behavior. People stop believing in you or taking you seriously, and the legitimate arguments of racism, discrimination, and prejudice become diluted by the bullshit ones thrown out by desperate defense attorneys. That's the thing that outrages me more than anything, and it took these two cases to set me down the path of righteous exasperation on this one issue.

Obviously, I don't expect defense attorneys to stop crying wolf on my say-so alone, but I do believe our prosecutors should allow themselves a little more room in calling attention to the ploy. Sometimes we're all just a little too timid, a little too politically correct, and we dance around sensitive issues like discrimination when what we should be doing is confronting them and dealing with them honestly. That's one of the reasons I love doing a show like *The View*. I lay it out there. Meredith and I have talked about this issue several times. We speak candidly. We discuss race like we discuss life. It *is* life. So let's start calling 'em like we see 'em, and telling it like it is. We've got to help the smoke clear a little bit if we want the truth to reveal itself. Like most people, I want to see an end to racism and sexism and every other kind of discrimination, but if we shrink from these frivolous charges we're gone as a society. We're just gone.

Lottie, Dottie, and Everybody

❦

You're used to dealing with rapists, murderers, and other criminals, but now that you're in television news, you're about to really see what evil is.
—NBC NEWS DIRECTOR DAVID VERDI,
on my first day of work at the network

WHEN YOU'RE A prosecutor, it's pretty clear you're a public servant. It's clear that your boss is an elected official. It's clear that if you botch too many cases and the bad guys are left to run wild in the streets, your boss will be voted out of office, and your butt won't be too far behind. You know precisely where the lines are drawn when you're a public servant. You know what's right and just, and what you need to do to keep your job.

Sometimes, things are a little less clear when you

work in the news media. In fact, a lot of people on the outside looking in may think there aren't any lines at all —other than the bottom line, that is. On the one hand there is the media, great and strong, speaking for all of us, standing for all of us, investigating our issues, and exposing that which can hurt us. But there can be a dark side. Some people who purport to be journalists treat this sacred trust as an anything-goes kind of business. For them, it's whatever you can get away with, as opposed to whatever's right and just. It's pushing the boundaries of ethics and propriety until you no longer recognize them. It's running with the story for as long as it lets you, until it finally runs away and you move on to the next one.

Ours is an ever-evolving world. We live now in an era of immediate news and information. No one has to wait anymore until six-thirty in the evening to see what Peter Jennings is going to say. You can turn on MSNBC any time of day, or CNN. You can log onto the Internet. There's no longer any reason to wait for the thud of the morning paper landing on your front stoop to get your daily fix. You can find out everything that's happened in the world up until about ten minutes ago, and in ten minutes you can find out the rest. It's all there in an instant. Just add water and stir.

Ah, but it's not so simple. The glitch to all this real-time access to breaking news is the hand-in-hand competition for some news organizations to get on the air or on the newsstand first with whatever new piece of information comes their way. It doesn't seem to matter if that information is important, or even if it's accurate, as long as they report it before anyone else. The veteran journalists tell me we've come a long way from how it was. A generation ago, newspaper reporters wrote their stories to fit a certain number of column inches, and to meet a fixed deadline. An editor determined how important a story was, and when it was due, and how much information there was available, and the reporter set off to fulfill the assignment. These days, journalists have the ability to get out with a story pretty much as it breaks, which usually means they're going to issue their accounts pretty much before they've completed their reporting—before the story has even fully unfolded. There are no real deadlines, as we first came to understand the term, just as there are no longer any fixed news holes to fill; if a story's too long or too short, it doesn't really matter because our mediums are now elastic enough to accommodate whatever you've got. Sometimes all you need to build an audience is a juicy photo, or a scandalous headline.

Whenever I consider the evolving role of the news media in our society, I think of a great Glenn Close line from the Ron Howard movie *The Paper*. The script had one of the New York City tabloids going with a story implicating two black kids in a shooting, even though there was mounting evidence to suggest that these kids might not have been involved. The dilemma, for the Glenn Close character running the newspaper, was whether to sit on the story for twenty-four hours, to see if these suspects were indeed charged, or to run it now, while technically speaking the cops were still looking at them for the crime. Ultimately, Glenn Close uttered these famous words that should have sounded through American newsrooms like a wake-up call: "We don't have to be right tomorrow. We have to be right today.''

Even though this was a line from a movie, I find that kind of thinking reprehensible, and yet we see it all the time in real life. In the race to be first, some of our leading news organizations have increasingly sacrificed the public trust in the interest of their bottom lines— and in the totally arbitrary interest of competition. I'm sorry, but I don't think the average viewer or reader gives a rat's tail whether or not their favorite news source has been *first* on the most stories. What counts is being *accurate* on the most stories. What counts is getting it right, and keeping the public trust. Newspapers, network and cable news shows, syndicated news programs, electronic news-gatherers . . . the impulse is virtually the same across the board, and the lines have yet to be redrawn. This troubles me, and it should trouble you. We *do* have to be right tomorrow —absolutely!—and if we can't be right tomorrow then we sure as hell should have *tried* to be right tomorrow. For all of you news media types out there reading this, saying what I heard some anchor say recently—''You critics have months to review what it takes us journalists seconds to decide'': bullshit. That applies to cops, firefighters, and rescue workers who hold life and death in their hands. What's the penalty for waiting until you have the facts right? You'll get beat by another news outlet. You get scooped. The bomb doesn't drop and people don't run wild in the streets. Life goes on. So don't go giving me that line. It doesn't jive.

To many people, the poster boy for our technology-driven rush to judgment is Richard Jewell, the man who was falsely accused of the bombing in the Olympic Village in Atlanta. By the time newspaper and television reporters were finished with him, Jewell couldn't leave his house. He was as guilty as the person responsible, because that's what the headlines told us. That was the lead story on the nightly news, and the hot topic of conversation on the cable talk shows. It got to where there were even Richard Jewell jokes being swapped around watercoolers across the country. There was no question, this was the guy. And yet, let's just suppose, in the time it took for him to be vindicated, some nut job with an ax to grind because his wife was killed in a years-ago bombing decided to shoot Richard Jewell to death as some twisted retribution. It could have happened. It could happen still. Despite the retractions, despite the public apologies from leading news organizations, as well as from the FBI and every other law enforcement agency involved in the case, Richard Jewell was forever branded as the "Olympic Bomber," and his life will never be the same. *"Whoops. Sorry, Mr. Jewell. We seem to have dropped the ball on this one. Would a lifetime subscription to the* Atlanta Journal and Constitution *make it up to you? What about if we throw in free cable?"*

Now, I'm no fool; somebody would've told me by now if I were. I understand that stories change, that what is accurate one moment can be inaccurate the next. What I don't understand, however, is the way some folks in the media play fast and loose with the truth and hide behind the safety net of a retraction, or a follow-up story reporting a contrary development. Too often, the thinking seems to mirror that in *The Paper.*

You know, if we can't get it right today, we can always fix it tomorrow. But you can't always fix it tomorrow, and there is evidence of this simple truth all around. Matt Drudge, whose Drudge Report is perhaps the most widely read electronic news service in Washington, D.C., can change his mind on a story every twenty minutes. But at least *he* cops to the fact that he is reporting rumor and innuendo. When Dallas Cowboys wide receiver Michael Irvin was accused of raping a Texas woman, it was front-page news across the country, even though police had never filed an arrest warrant. When he was cleared in the matter, it made headlines primarily in Dallas; almost everywhere else, it was a back-of-the-sports-pages blurb. And the fact that the female "victim" pled guilty to perjury after implicating Irvin was hardly reported at all.

Sometimes there's nothing you can do to restore a person's reputation. In Irvin's case, he'd had his share of screwups, so folks weren't too broken up about sullying an already tarnished reputation, but that seemed to me to be beside the point. The point, really, was that the man didn't do what the news accounts had him doing. His innocence was never reported in the same manner, or with the same fervor, as the allegations against him, and to the few of us who even bothered to notice, there was nothing to do but scratch our heads and think, Well, that's just the way it goes sometimes.

Excuse me, but that shouldn't be the way it goes, sometimes or anytime, and most of the respected journalists I talked to agree. The pros all criticize any story that is reported before it's thoroughly sourced and investigated. Is it enough to say that such-and-such was reported in the *Daily Planet*? Who the hell knows if we can trust the *Daily Planet*?

Here's another example. In the aftermath of Princess Diana's terrible car crash, all kinds of ridiculous things were being reported before they could be checked out. The accident, you'll recall, happened over a weekend, and many Americans stayed up all night watching the news, once they'd been tipped to the story. I'll never forget it. I was at my parents' house, and I was glued to the television. It was a powerful, emotional story, and for a news junkie like me, it was also one of those rare, riveting moments when most every station, in most parts of the country, switched to live, breaking coverage. I flipped from one channel to the next, and watched through bleary-teary eyes as the princess's final moments were discussed and analyzed by so-called "people in the know." Trouble was, some of the talking heads doing this round-the-clock discussing and analyzing were very clearly in the don't-know. During one stretch, I was watching MSNBC, and the anchor announced that he'd just received a call from the Paris or London bureau chief of a major national newsmagazine. MSNBC immediately patched the call in and broadcast the caller live before checking it out any further. The "bureau chief" then reported that Princess Diana and Dodi Al-Fayed were en route to a video store at the time of the crash. The reason they were driving at a high rate of speed, according to this source, was that they were trying to get to the store before it closed in order to rent the Howard Stern movie *Private Parts*. This actually went out over the damn television!

Live! In an effort to beat everybody else with a breaking news story, a reputable news outlet was willing to cut a few corners and ignore the obvious. I laughed like a fool.

In this case, there was no real harm done by the misinformation (other than to embarrass MSNBC in the short term), and by the end of the night there were a dozen other examples of sloppy reporting from a dozen other news organizations, but the gaffe was emblematic. In the race to be first, and fast, we report every angle, no matter how obtuse, simply because we can. If we go to press in one minute, or if we're on the air in five, or if our electronic subscribers are anxiously awaiting our next posting, we reporters tell ourselves we have to go out with something, because there's nothing worse than dead air or blank space or being beaten on a story.

Something tells me we're better than that, and here again I go back to my days as a prosecutor, when getting a conviction was not always the goal. Yes, I wanted to win, but not at all costs. As soon as I lost the arrogance of youth I realized it was more important to do the right thing. Justice always outs in the end, I learned—and when it doesn't, it's better to err on the side of certainty. I would rather that a hundred bad guys go free than one good guy put away for something he didn't do, and in my less than humble opinion, we have to extend that kind of thinking to our news organizations. I would rather see a hundred unverified stories go unreported than one false lead allowed into print. I'm sorry, but I would rather that a hundred lunatics light their dogs on fire on a Los Angeles freeway, *beyond* the glare of the television cameras, than see one local station cut into afternoon children's programming with live coverage.

I am not alone in this. More and more, I'm starting to hear a loud cry against some of the standard tactics of even our most respected news organizations. Network news divisions. Major dailies. All have now rushed to report a story that ten years ago would never have seen newsprint or made it on the air. As a prosecutor, I had to come forward to a grand jury with probable cause just to get an indictment, and those same checks and balances need to be in place in our news organizations, no matter what technology allows us to do. In some cases—indeed, in most cases—there are checks and balances, it's just that they're adopted on a purely voluntary basis. At the *New York Times,* for example, there's an editorial board that in one way or another determines whether each story is worthy of the paper's reputation. The same thing happens at ABC News. In some ways, I guess, the same thing happens at the *National Enquirer.* In some newsrooms, there are policies in place requiring reporters to double- or triple-source their facts before running with a story. In others, a single source is all you need. And, in lesser newsrooms, all it takes is for a little birdie to whisper something into a reporter's ear for a salacious piece of information to find its way into print, or onto videotape. The bar changes from one newsroom to the next. But I would venture to say that even our highest standards have been lowered in recent years.

And what has been the upshot of this decline? Well, for one thing, it has changed the stakes for our elected officials, and for other prominent individuals in government, business, and entertainment. We now live in a world where public people can no longer lead private lives, and I think that's a shame. In my own case, I've always tried to live my life in such a way that I wouldn't be embarrassed if anything I'd done was reported on *60 Minutes*, but I've always been that way. Even before my television career put me in the public eye, I was careful not to behave in such a way that what I did the night before would lead the morning news. I would not humiliate myself, or my family. That's one of the reasons I've never smoked dope or taken 'ludes or snorted cocaine or any of those little hip things some people my age have done. Not once. Why? Because it's illegal and irresponsible. I felt it then, and I feel it now. I wanted to be a lawyer. I wanted to stand in a courtroom and uphold the law, and I didn't want to be looking over my shoulder wondering if some shoe was going to drop on my career.

Still, there are good, smart people who make stupid choices in their lives, and now we have made it so that those stupid choices come back to bite them in the butt, big-time. But what about those good, smart people who've lived good, smart lives and avoided those stupid choices? For a lot of them, it's no longer worth it to seek the light of a public career. Look at someone like Colin Powell, a man who has been a great leader and who can undoubtedly be an even greater one. He puts people first. He values God and family. He's dedicated to America. And yet there is no way he's going to subject his family and friends to the media grind of a political career, and that is a shame. It's a shame on us all.

And what about those public people whose private tragedies are trotted out for public consumption? Arthur Ashe was essentially forced to step forward and announce that he was infected with HIV when it became clear that *USA Today* was about to "break" his story. More recently, Carly Simon had to disclose her breast cancer because a tabloid was set to tell the world. How despicable is it that we trade on the miseries of people simply because they're famous?

What's interesting is that there seems to be a whole different attitude among news media regarding celebrities and politicians. Have you noticed this, or is it just me? News organizations do not actively seek to tear down our pop culture celebrities. (Unless of course you happen to be poor Frank Gifford.) In some ways, you could argue, they actually look to build them up, but if you take one misstep they'll start selling tickets to watch you fall. (Especially if you happen to be Frank Gifford.) If some illness or other tragedy should strike you or your family, they'll camp out on your front lawn and watch you suffer. Oh, they might be rooting for you to come through the ordeal happier and healthier than ever before, but they don't want to be caught napping in case you succumb to whatever it is that's got your number. With politicians, however, I think they're out there gunning from the very beginning. They're looking for the bad stuff, and willing you to fail.

Think about it: We've allowed our news media to take us to the point where, in our next national election, we will probably be asking candidates, "Have you ever had an extramarital affair?" This will become our new litmus test; in many ways, it already has. Of course, there's only one right answer: "None of your damn business." We can ask if they've ever assaulted someone, if they've ever sexually harassed someone, if they've ever committed a crime. These things are our business, citizens. But whether or not a person has had an indiscretion in his or her marriage is out of bounds. It's *way* out of bounds.

The question was put to Dan Quayle, on *Meet the Press*, during his never-ending trial-balloon quest for the next Republican presidential nomination, and he danced around it. He said he didn't think it was an appropriate question to ask a politician, but he answered no anyway. I wanted to throw a brick through the television. Really, the man could have knocked it out of the damn park, if he'd simply said it wasn't anybody's business but Marilyn's, but wussy Dan Quayle went at it from what he thought was the correct view.

So this is what's on the table now, and I'm waiting for the next bellwether question for our female candidates: "Have you ever had an abortion?" Tell me that's not going to happen. And soon. And when it does, I hope to God the woman has the strength of character to take that microphone from the reporter's hand and smash it to the floor, because once you open that door a hard rain's gonna come. That's how we got into this ridiculous mess in the first place. It was Gary Hart, opening the damn door. He told reporters he wasn't fooling around on his wife, and then he invited them to come and catch him fooling around on his wife. How stupid can one person be? He opened the door. It's just like in a courtroom. A judge can keep evidence out. She can keep testimony out. She can keep certain facts from the jury. But once you open the door, once your stupid witness opens his stupid mouth and triggers that open-door policy, all of it comes in. And that's what happened. Gary Hart opened the door, and now we have to listen to whether or not the president of the United States has a hard-on in a little cubby next to the Oval Office, crunching some girl up against a wall like he's some seventeen-year-old debate-team geek trying to get his rocks off in the hallway of his high school. Honestly, I am so sick of people wanting to know how many times Monica Lewinsky was in the White House, how many presents she received from the president, how many calls were logged by Clinton's secretary. Please! People in hell want ice water and they don't get it. So mind your business and let the case play out in court, or run out of steam, and unless or until someone presents some credible evidence to the contrary, let's give the president the benefit of the doubt (that is the law, isn't it) and leave him alone to do his job.

This is what we've become. This is where we've allowed our news organizations to take us. And soon we'll have to consider the image of a fine and worthy female candidate with her legs up in stirrups in some abortion clinic, because the question will be put to her and she won't know how to answer it. Believe me, that day is coming, but I hope another one gets here first. I long for the day when a candidate or celebrity will turn the question back on their interviewer, and ask how many times he's stepped out on his wife or cheated on his taxes. Baby, I will watch television on *that* day, for certain.

I don't need this. We don't need this. It's just T.M.I.—Too Much Information. Actually, it's T.M.*F.*I. Literally. And I suppose we only have ourselves to blame. The media wouldn't put it out there for us to consider if we weren't lapping this stuff up, and if I'm being completely honest about it I should 'fess to some of my own lapping. I was right there, with all the rest of you, watching O. J. and A. C. driving that Bronco along the 405. I was glued to that tube. And what was it I was expecting to see? In the deepest, darkest recesses of my imagination, where images alight in my head that I don't even want to think about, I knew full well what might happen. I watched to see if O. J. was going to shoot himself, same as you. Don't try telling me America watched that chase to see O. J. pull into his driveway and wave hello to the television cameras and ask, "What's for dinner?" It was a soap opera—a tragic, desperate soap opera. And we all knew how it could end. Not how it *would* end, but how it *could*. We weren't necessarily hoping it would end badly, but we were waiting for it.

If we didn't ingest this stuff like candy, they wouldn't put it on the air. If Lottie, Dottie, and everybody didn't want to be in your business, these shows and newspapers would do a slow fade. If those tabloid newspapers didn't jump off the racks at our supermarkets, they wouldn't carry the same weight and power.

If we didn't shell out our hard-earned money to watch Pamela Anderson's kinky home movies, it wouldn't have been one of the top-selling video titles of 1997. (My confession on this one is that I would never have gone and bought the tape, but if someone popped a copy in the VCR at the office or at some party, I would have definitely watched.)

When I worked for the syndicated program *Inside Edition* covering the Simpson trial, I was sensitive to charges of "tabloid journalism." It bristled me and, in all honesty, made me defensive. Why? Because I knew that for the most part the people at *Inside,* like others in the news gathering business, were trying to do their jobs well. No one in the business of journalism is out there trying to get it wrong. But it is imperative that those trying to get it right step up to the plate.

I sometimes wonder what would happen if the *Star* and the *Enquirer* just disappeared off our radar screens. Would we miss them? Would it change the way we think, the way we love, the way we look at the world? Would it change us in some fundamental way? Yeah, probably, but only in good ways, don't you think? This shared impulse to sell people out and trip 'em up would just vanish. We'd stop rooting for people to fail and start rooting for them to succeed. (Hey, what a concept!) We'd start demanding more of our news organizations by turning away from the ones that can't seem to get their stories right, the ones for whom the race to be first circumvents the commitment to be accurate. We'd understand the differences among what we have a right to know, what we have a wish to know, and what we have a need to know. We'd separate the prurient interest from the public interest. And we'd look at ourselves in the mirror and start to question—really question—what it means for a free and unfettered press to be right today, and tomorrow, and for all time.

It's Not Who You Are, but What You Wear

❦

There are only two types of women—

goddesses and doormats.

—PABLO PICASSO

FORGIVE ME, BUT I just love that title.

Now, a word of caution: Do not, I repeat, do not read this chapter in a vacuum. I am *not* a self-absorbed little ninny who only cares about being the Grand Duchess. But when I am given the chance (and this book is that chance) to take a flight of fancy and bring you along, I've gotta be over the top . . . you wouldn't expect less. So come along with me on my journey to the world of a diva.

We've gone back and forth in this book up till now,

from serious to not-so-serious, and we'll continue to do so, but I feel like having a little fun over the next few pages. With that in mind, let me set out the term *diva* as I've tried to redefine it. A diva is a woman with a Delightfully Interesting, Vivacious Attitude. Sound like someone you know?

Damn straight, I'm a diva, and I've got the attitude to prove it. I've also got the shoes, so let's start there. About three hundred pairs, bought and paid for and occasionally even worn. Out of that three hundred there're maybe thirty that will never again see the light of day, but I've got 'em. More than that, I've got a place to keep 'em. One of the best things about being on television is that you've got a place to store some of your clothing purchases when you run out of closets at home. You've got a wardrobe room, and there's no point being a diva unless you've got a wardrobe room.

I'm a diva from the tips of my toes to the top of my head. Can I tell you about my hair? Black women obsess about their hair. And it's not just *this* black woman. We're all guilty, and this is one of those times when a broad generalization will not get me beaten up. (One morning on *The View,* Meredith suggested that women always obsess about their weight. "Meredith," I said, "it's only white women who obsess about their weight. Black women obsess about their hair.") Go ahead, try talking me down from this one. Hair is *it* to a black woman concerned about her appearance. Do we want it in its natural state, which can tend to be fairly curly? Do we want to relax it, make it straighter, buy a little bit into the European ideal of what hair should look like on a woman? Or do we do some kind of combination, and get the hair weaves, and the wigs, and the extensions? There's always something going on with our hair, always something to worry about, some new thing to try. Believe me, I've tried every conceivable look. About the only thing I haven't done is go natural, because that's a look that doesn't go well with my hair, and if it doesn't go well with my hair, it doesn't belong on my head.

I've had my hair relaxed since I was nine. I started straightening it at about six—or, I should say, I started having it straightened. It was a passive act, back then. It's a rite of passage for a little black girl, sitting in her mother's kitchen on a little stool, with a straightening comb on the burner. There's always some grease on the back of the mother's left hand, and she takes the grease and rubs it into the edges of the hair, and then she takes the hot comb and goes to it. If it wasn't my mother it was one of my grandmothers, or an aunt. I'm telling you, every female relative had her hands in my hair at one point or another, and it was the same way for every little black girl I knew. We all had our hair straightened. Every week. For me it was always on Saturday. I washed my hair and took my place on the stool in the kitchen and sat back and waited for the smell of my hair frying to fill the small room. If you've never smelled that smell, it'll trip you out.

Nowadays, we don't use a burner from the stove. Somebody has invented this little electric oven thing that has taken its place. Joy calls it my Easy-Bake oven. When we were auditioning hairstylists for the show, the one thing I insisted on was someone who could straighten my hair with one of those ovens. It was actually a sticking point in my contract, because the people in the Business Affairs office at ABC didn't realize they were dealing with a diva whose hair is as important as her law degree.

At nine, I got a relaxer, or a perm, as we called it in the neighborhood. The relaxer was this chemical compound we used to buy, and it smelled so foul it could curl your eyelashes. Aw, it was disgusting! And the lye-based relaxers could actually burn you if you weren't careful. It's amazing, the hoops we jumped through just to get our hair straight, but there was never any question that this was what I was gonna do. That first Easter, when I got my first perm, I was the queen. I was so happy. I didn't care how it smelled, or how it burned, or how long it took. I loved having straight hair. It was all so sophisticated. So grown-up. Stop! Wait a minute—before we go too far down this path, I don't want any little girls reading this to think that you need straight hair to be beautiful. You don't—it's just that, at nine, that's what I wanted. As long as you've got hair that you like, that looks good and makes you *feel* beautiful, then you are beautiful and don't let anyone tell you different.

These days, since I started working in television, I've become a major wig person. Wigs give us divas a whole bunch of fashion options, but there's a practical benefit to them as well. When you're a black woman on television, and someone else is doing your hair while you're getting your wardrobe straight and going over your notes, it's not like being back in Shirley's kitchen on a Saturday afternoon. You don't have all the time in the world, or even all the tools you need to do the job right. I'm lucky to have Marqué and Deirdre (my Emmy-winning hairstylists at *The View*), but most of the hairstylists who work in the business don't have the utensils I like to use on my hair—straightening combs, blow-dryers that really blow my hair dry, rollers made for *my* hair. If I didn't have wigs as an alternative, I'd have to go on television looking a little tacky, and the kid is not going to go on television looking tacky. I'm sorry, but that's not an option.

It may start with the hair, but it ends with the clothes. For a woman who wears over a size twelve, there are things you want to accentuate and some things you want to hide, depending on your body type. I have great legs, so I'm always looking to show them off. But I don't wear short skirts on television, because there is a time and a place for everything. (You divas in training, take note.) The last thing I want is my skirt hiking up on me while I'm on live television, and me pulling and adjusting and looking all awkward and flustered. (Make a note of this too: awkward and flustered . . . not good things.)

I love wearing one of those clingy Marc Bouwer evening gowns, 'cause, baby, I look good in sexy evening clothes. I also have a killer chest, so I look for outfits that highlight that area as well, but I won't wear anything low-cut. Remember, I've got that nasty scar from my surgery back in college, and if I call attention to it with a low-cut top, I'm asking people to make it into a topic of conversation, so I go another way. I put a whole look together. I accentuate the face, the hair, the legs. . . . There's an ensemble thing happening, and at the base of it is my makeup. I wear makeup all the time, whenever I leave the house, and lately I've been making myself up almost as well as Alan and Karim, the makeup artists on the show. Put me at a Mac or Iman counter at closing time, and I'll make it worth the manager's while to stay open long enough for me to make a purchase.

What helps the makeup stand out is tonal dressing underneath. I look good in color. This is what people tell me—but a true diva doesn't need to be told what makes her look good. She knows. The purples, the reds, the fuchsias, the yellows, the oranges . . . I can wear all those colors, and I do, but I'll typically save the bright-bright tones for a jacket. I like a monochromatic look—say, a matching trouser and blouse set off by a different-color blazer. Or I'll match the blouse and the jacket and go for a different-color trouser. I'll mix it up. I'll even wear all three pieces the same, but what I won't do is mix lots and lots of color. It doesn't do to look like you're trying too hard. People should notice you in the clothes, and not the clothes on you, if you know what I mean. I'll sometimes let an accessory make an impression. I believe in jewelry, but I won't wear delicate pieces that get lost on me. I'm a big girl, so I don't wear tiny earrings. I wear bold earrings. Not tacky, flamboyant earrings—just big enough and bold enough to kinda help announce my arrival. I'll wear a necklace and a bracelet and a pair of earrings and that'll be fine, but you won't see me topping that outfit off with a pin and a scarf. For my money, less is more, so on days when I want to wear a pin or a scarf I'll lose the necklace or the bracelet.

If you look back at our first year of *The View*, you'll

see I've never worn the same outfit twice (thanks to Fran and Julie, the best stylists on earth). Nobody cares about this but me, but I do care. I do. How I present myself, whether it's on television or on the town, is important to me. I've mixed and matched, I've worn the same blouse or the same blazer, but there's always something different going on, something new. Of course, it's almost an unfair claim to say that I wear a different outfit to work every day, because most people don't have the resources available to me as one of the cohosts of a network television program. I recognize that. There are all kinds of designers and jewelry manufacturers and wig makers and cosmetics companies trying to get us to wear their products on the show, so there are all kinds of choices. Plus, I'm making the kind of salary that allows me to indulge myself in this area, and I know too well that real people, in real jobs, don't always have that luxury, but I was this way about my wardrobe back when I was working in Brooklyn, making $22,500.

I spent way too much of my public servant's salary on clothes, but I made sure my money went a good long way. I couldn't afford a real Chanel scarf, but I knew where they sold the fakes on Canal Street in lower Manhattan. I couldn't afford to go to a Fifth Avenue hair salon, but the Dominican girls uptown in Spanish Harlem could do my hair for fourteen dollars a week, and they still give the best perms in the city, at any price. I didn't have the means, but I had the style. Baby, I always had the style. Even then, I'd try never to wear the same outfit twice, in front of the same jury. And people picked up on it. Once, when I was putting the fairly complex Crown Heights hit-and-run case that sparked a citywide race riot into the grand jury, the jurors started referring to me as the Chairman of the Fashion Police. They took bets on how long I could go without repeating an outfit, and it was three and a half weeks before we were through.

I could have gone another month.

Every female prosecutor in our office had her special summation outfit. The men too. They all had their favorite suits, or their lucky ties, and we had our trusty ensembles that couldn't help but send the right message to the judge and jury. For me, in winter, it was always a black suede bugle skirt. Man, that was a killer skirt! It flared nicely at the bottom, and reached pretty much down to my ankles, and I set it off with a pair of high-heeled take-me-home-and-do-me black pumps, because you've got to give 'em the chick thing. (I don't care how good an attorney you are, the chick thing never hurts.) On top, I usually wore a brown-and-black jacket that was longer than most jackets—it came down over my rear end—but it looked completely great on me, and underneath I always had a black turtleneck sweater.

The outfit came with a classic move: At some key point in the trial (which usually coincided with when it started to get hot in the courtroom), I took off my jacket and continued on in my sweater, which of course nicely highlighted the great Star Jones chest. Let me tell you, a lot of people went to jail on that outfit. It sent the right message. It said, This girl has got it going on. She looks good. She knows she looks good. Let's listen to what she has to say.

I think clothes should convey a message, don't you?

It doesn't matter if you're prosecuting a case, or interviewing someone on television, or running down to the corner store for some eggs and milk, your clothes are the best billboard to your personality. I'm always thinking, What am I going for here? I think about how I'm feeling, how I want to be seen, and then I dress to suit. I play a little game with my girlfriends. I tell them to give me a mood or an emotion, and off the top of my head I describe an outfit to match, one that goes along with my size, my shape, and my style. Just one word and I know what I'm wearing.

Outgoing? Purple suede pants. Purple cashmere turtleneck. Hermès scarf tied at the neck, with maybe purple, black, and white as the combination of colors. High-heeled black leather boots. Cuff bracelet, with matching earrings. No necklace.

Demure? A long, floral peasant dress, down to the ankles. It should be the kind of soft silk floral that flows on you, almost like a sundress. Strappy sandals. Not flat, but not too high—maybe two inches off the ground. Hair pulled back with a barrette in a ponytail at the base of the neck. A chignon. Light jewelry. Pearl drop earrings. And one of those cute, hip necklaces with the tiny pearls connected to the gold chain and the little pearl drop coming down in the center.

Aggressive? Well, that's my summation suit. I've got that one committed to routine, because this diva is always aggressive. Outside the courtroom, you can maybe dress it up with a long pendant piece of jewelry, and flat gold earrings. Maybe find a long blazer in a vibrant color. And hair. This is an outfit that needs sophisticated hair.

Sexy? Sexy is a white silk evening dress, topped with a white chiffon see-through duster coat. Hair piled way high on your head in a slightly messy look, or what I would call the F.F. look—as in freshly "done." Open, high-heeled strappy sandals, with a toe ring. Left foot or right foot, it doesn't matter, but it should be the second toe, the pointer toe. Maybe it's just me, but a toe ring always gets me going.

Uncertain? Please, this is Star. There's no such thing as uncertain. If it's uncertainty you mean to convey, then pull up those covers, turn on the T.V., watch my girl Erica Kane, who is never uncertain, and stay the heck in bed. Even in a courtroom setting, there was never any room for uncertain. Either you've got the goods or you don't, and if I didn't have the goods I would not have been in the courtroom, so let's just move on to the next one, okay?

Fabulous? Red silk palazzo pants, with a matching red silk duster coat that buttons down the front. The buttons should reach down to where the pants meet, and the coat should have some flare to it. High-heeled red shoes, and a huge red chiffon scarf that flows when you walk. That's fabulous.

I also wear fur. I know a lot of people don't approve of it, but I like the feel of a mink coat. I won't wear the fur of any endangered species, because I think that's irresponsible. My opinion. My right. And I respect your right not to wear any fur at all. I respect your right to be antifur or anti—anything else you want to be, so long as you respect my right to disagree with you. Respect my right to wear what I choose, and don't be in my face screaming about my fur coat with your leather shoes and belt and snakeskin purse over your arm. Those items come from animal skins, same as mine. And while we're on it, don't come to me with brown roots and blond streaks and a face full of makeup that has been tested on laboratory animals. Also, some of that medicine you need to take for your allergies, your heart, your pain has been made available by the Food and Drug Administration only after it was tested on animals.

No diva should make excuses for wearing fur, because she doesn't have to. I don't even resent people telling me their opinion on the matter. What I do resent are people who think that I have to share their opinion, or that I should lie about it because they believe it's "socially correct" to do so. And don't you even think about throwing something on me or assaulting me when you see me out in my mink coat, because I will forget for that one moment that I am a law-abiding citizen and an officer of the court and I will kick your butt. Be clear.

Now, while we're having fun in the fantasy world of a diva, let's move on to the one fashion accessory that goes with any outfit—the right set of wheels. Even in New York, you need to pull up with style. If you're driving yourself, a sporty Cadillac says something. But when being driven, a limousine will accomplish this for you nicely, but it has to be the right limousine. I won't get into one of those tacky white limousines unless I have to, because they always make me feel like a mobster, or the girlfriend of one of those snakeskin pimps singing about cars with a diamond cut out in the back and a sun roof top. That's just tacky. If I have to ride in one, I'll have the driver drop me off around the corner. One of those classy Mercedes limousines is a far more elegant and understated choice, preferably in silver, or black if that's all they've got. A cherry red sport utility vehicle will nicely complement our outgoing ensemble, and a silver Mercedes sedan won't clash with demure or cocky or sexy or fabulous. But you want to stay out of those long white limos—unless you're going to your junior prom.

I have more clothes than most boutiques, and I can throw any one of these looks together at a moment's notice. This isn't necessarily a good thing or a bad thing, but it's my thing. It's what I do, and for people who don't obsess about their sense of style but still want to look great there are some neat shortcuts available to everyone. I always tell women to buy a pile of fashion magazines and start thumbing through with an eye toward the various moods and emotions you want to convey. Don't look at the models. Whatever you do, don't look at the models. Cut off their heads if you have to. Put little mustaches on them, so you don't think about the things they've got going on that you can't quite manage. Keep the focus on the clothes, on the style. Write down what you like about that dress or that outfit, what each outfit conveys: outgoing, demure, sexy. . . . And then cut these pictures out and tape them to the wall in your closet, and when you're going for a certain look you'll have something to pattern yourself after. No, not everybody can afford the designer fashions I'm lucky enough to get from The Forgotten Woman, the great Marc Bouwer, or one of those high-end numbers you'll find in the fashion magazines. But you can always go to JC Penney or Sears or Lane Bryant or The Limited or a fabulous outlet and get a nice little knockoff. (I'll let you in on a little secret: That's still where I do a lot of my serious shopping. I know the Gucci outlet's number by heart!)

What it comes down to, though, is not the clothes, but the attitude you wear beneath them. It's about commanding attention. If you're gonna strut, then strut. If you're gonna diva, then diva. (Hell, it's *my* book, and if I want to turn the word *diva* into a verb, it's gonna take more than a stodgy old copy editor to stop me!) We divas know something the rest of the world doesn't, and I'll let you in on it: People, for some reason, get off on "over the top" people. I don't know what it is, or why it is, but it absolutely is. Think about it. Think about the over-the-top, larger-than-life, holier-than-thou people you know in your life, and think about the kind of stuff they get away with. Think about what *you* let them get away with. I think all the time about what I get away with in my life, and it tickles the palazzo pants off of me. I find I don't wait in lines. I don't wait for tables in a crowded restaurant. I don't have to take no for an answer. And the reason I don't have to do any of these things has nothing to do with the fact that I'm on television, or the fact that I dress a certain way; it has to do with how I carry myself. It has to do with who I am.

I know some people might take one look at who I am and how I carry myself and call me a bitch. Perhaps, to them, I am. Some people might say I was just sure of my place. This is true. I don't think there's any place for me but the top. I belong at the top of whatever I'm doing, and I don't feel I belong there at the expense of anyone else's being there. You can be at the top too. I'm willing to share. There's plenty of room at the top. Who wants to be at the bottom?

It really is all about attitude. When I call down to the superintendent of my building to report a leaky faucet or some other plumbing problem, I'll put on my most pleasant and at the same time most demanding voice and ask, "What time can I expect you to come up and fix it?" I won't ask the man if he will come up. Whether he will or he won't isn't even an issue. He will. I've already told him so. Now the only issue is what time, and if I really wanted to be bold about it I could say, "What time between one and three in the afternoon can I expect you?" But you've got to work up to that. Don't start right out of the box with such bold strokes.

The trick is to go about getting what it is you think you're entitled to, without coming across as, well . . . entitled. I'm never entitled in a way that puts people off. At least, I don't think I am. I'm always nice to people who are doing nice things for me— whether it's my super in the building, or a waiter in a restaurant, or one of the production assistants at the studio. Even a diva knows that the feet you step on today are usually connected to the ass you will kiss tomorrow. I always keep that in mind. Being a diva is not being a bitch. Being a diva is fun, and it offers a great vantage point on the world. The view from the top is a whole lot better than the view from the bottom, don't you think?

I was a diva at two years old. I wouldn't wear pants

to play outside. I always wanted my hair done and my fingers clean. Shirley says I was the most fastidious little girl she'd ever seen. I was constantly running in and out of the kitchen, washing my hands in the sink. I was weird like that. Still, to this day, I've got to be clean. Little girls have got to be clean. I see a pretty little girl walking down the street with some ice cream or something dripping down her chin and I just want to grab a napkin and clean her face. Child, that just won't do.

And yet for all my refinement, I'm a fairly self-reliant person. I know how to use a hammer, how to change a tire, how to wire my stereo. It's just that I choose not to. I'm not the type to paint my apartment, or change the oil in my car, even though I can probably manage those simple tasks just fine. It's just not me, and as long as I have the resources to not have to do these things, there's no way I'm going to. Anyway, a true diva wouldn't be caught dead cleaning out the garage. I'm the handiest girl you're likely to meet, but I put it to work on an as-needed basis. Why should I get out and fix my car on the side of the road? I've got my cellular phone. I've got my roadside assistance. It doesn't prove my womanhood to be able to jump-start my own car, or change a flat tire. Proving my womanhood is being able to get AAA to come and do it for me. I don't have to prove anything to anybody. I'm a full-fledged, card-carrying diva. It's *you* who needs to prove something to *me*.

As I set these thoughts to paper, however, I realize my diva-ness is probably my security blanket, to get me through life. I'll admit it's as much something to hide behind as it is something to get out in front about. It's kinda like my game face, my acting the diva; it's the way I look at the world, and the way I want the world to look back.

But it's Star who's the diva, and it's Starlet who's the person. My mother doesn't know me as Star. My family doesn't know me as Star. To them, I'm Starlet. Let Star have her diva thing, but Starlet is a little bit different. I'm quieter and gentler. I can be vulnerable and shy. I'm protective of my family. I'm fiercely loyal. I'm sure of myself, but I'm not always dead certain; there's room for discussion. My friend Vanessa knows us both. Star is the "Grand Duchess" who regales her with tales of the Ritz in Paris and the Swiss Riviera. But Starlet is her best friend who can talk to her for two hours on the phone about family and life and children and fears and hopes and dreams. There are softer edges to me than I show in my public life. There's champagne and caviar, but there's also Bud Light and pepperoni pizza, and there are times when I much prefer the latter. Take away the wigs and the eyelashes and the fabulous clothes, and you'll find me at White Castle, feasting on a half-dozen of those greasy square burgers. This ain't no metaphor. This is my treat. There's even a White Castle a few blocks from my apartment, with a drive-through window, and let me tell you, it's the perfect detour at the end of a perfectly glamorous day.

Just pretend not to notice if you see me pulling up in one of those tacky white limousines.

Strength of a Woman

❧

The greater the obstacle, the more
glory in overcoming it.
—MOLIÈRE

I DON'T KNOW if it's because I've been blessed,
or if it's because that's just how it is, but all of the
women in my life have been forces to be reckoned
with. Each and every one. If she's made an impact on
me, she's had something strong going on, something
big.

The list is rich, and it starts with my mother, Shirley. There're my grandmothers, Pauline and Muriel,
and my mother's eight sisters—Pearl, Elizabeth, Max-
ine, Evelyn, Doris, Nancy, Betty, and Evangeline.

There's Donald's sister, Shirley, and my own sister, Sheila. There are my older sorority sisters—Faye and Janet and far more than I can mention here . . . they *all* had a hand in making me the woman I am today. There was Dr. Betty Shabazz, Malcolm's widow, with whom I shared a too-brief friendship that lasted long enough for me to see what it was like to emerge at the other end of profound tragedy. There were two of my favorite judges, Priscilla Hall and Ruth Moskowitz, the former a strong black woman who will always stand as my legal ideal and the latter a tough, smart powerball who could command more attention than any woman had a right to. And there's Barbara Walters, my most recent friend and mentor, who casts perhaps the biggest shadow there is for a professional woman. These women took everything life threw at them and shined. Of course, they sometimes stumbled; some of them even fell down, but they didn't stay down long. I ascribe to them their own credo: "If you can look up, you can get up. And if you can get up, you can walk again."

And it hasn't just been the celebrated women in my life who have left their marks on me, or my own friends and family. Indeed, one of the biggest marks was left by a shy, unassuming young woman who stood at the center of one of my final cases in the Brooklyn DA's office. It was also one of my most memorable, and when I look back at that adrenaline-charged period in my professional life it stands out for all kinds of reasons.

Let me set the scene a bit before I tell the tale. . . .

During my last year in Brooklyn, I'd been tapped by District Attorney Charles "Joe" Hynes to join an elite group of prosecutors known informally around the office as "the trial cadre." He pulled me out of Homicide, where I had been trying cases for the previous two and a half years, promoted me to senior assistant district attorney, and started to assign me some of the more prominent cases to cross his desk. He did this, mind you, over the dead bodies of the women I fondly called the Bitches of Homicide. (Hey, if John Updike ever starts writing courtroom thrillers, that wouldn't be a bad title.) I'm sure you know the type—the women who don't have a nice word to say about anyone or anything; the ones who are so unhappy with their own lives that they begrudge you the happiness in yours. These women hated my guts, and resented the very air I breathed, and according to my good friends who remain on the job they're still not crazy about me. I was much younger than they were, and much louder, and in their minds no more deserving of the promotion than any of them, so they very kindly offered me their cold shoulders for the rest of my tenure there. I didn't mind. Actually, I found their resentment mildly amusing, and I'm happy to finally give them the attention they deserve in these pages. The Bitches of Homicide. They know who they are—and so do their colleagues.

Anyway, I was surrounded by a bunch of very talented prosecutors who were my main friends in the office—Paul Burns, Gary Farrell, Bruce McIntyre, Dan Saunders, and my principal partner in crime and all other things, John Riley. No kidding, if you were to look in the dictionary under *assistant district attorney,* I swear you'd find John's picture. He looks the part. Six foot two, blond hair, blue eyes, drop-dead gorgeous, and smart as hell. John and the other boys, along with some of the best detectives in Brooklyn, taught me much of what I know about being a prosecutor. I had the talent in the courtroom, but hanging with these boys taught me the skill. They taught me how to hold my own in front of a jury, using style and substance. They also taught me how to drink beer—several, actually.

I loved being an assistant in the office—prosecuting a full load of homicides, bringing high-profile cases before the grand jury and developing a reputation as one of the heavy-hitters in this elite group. At this senior level, Joe Hynes assigned us our cases personally, and he naturally tried to play to our strengths. What I was good at, I liked to think, were cases with a strong human element. I still wasn't practiced in the area of sex crimes—Homicide was my main beat—but every now and then a case fell to me that my bosses felt no one else could handle in just the same way. The trial of the serial offender known in the local media as the Bicycle Rapist was one of those cases.

As it is with most bad guys, this one was named for his modus operandi. His given name was William Gonzalez, and what he would do was ride his bicycle in front of a car driven by a woman and somehow arrange to be hit by the car. Then he would fall to the ground and pretend to be hurt. The woman would invariably step out of her car and offer help; in some instances, she might even offer the bicyclist a ride, whereupon he would pull a weapon and force her to a secluded place and rape her. From 1989 to 1991, our office built five cases against Gonzalez, and in the summer of 1991, it fell to me to try the last of the rapes. The first trial covered three victims, and the thinking was that it would be our strongest case. After all, when you have three victims who are going to come into a courtroom and identify the same man as the man who raped them, when those three victims have never met each other, when they all describe the same method, it should be a lock, or a "ground ball," as we used to say. It was not a question of force or no force. It was not acquaintance rape. It was stranger rape—a pure ID case—and the three corroborating testimonies should have put this bastard away, but something went wrong. That something was defense attorney Sam Gregory.

Sam—unfortunately for us, but fortunately for his defendants—was the best thing Legal Aid had going at the time, and one of the strongest lawyers I've ever seen. He knew how to create doubt where none should exist. He could take a compelling piece of evidence from the prosecution and poke it so full of holes you could feel a breeze running through it. Or he could take a flimsy piece of defense testimony and lace it with enough importance that the jurors would buy it. Put it this way: If you're reading this book and you're ever in trouble, Sam's wouldn't be a bad number for you to have. To get an acquittal on a triple rape—against the Brooklyn DA's office—was a great big deal.

If Sam received another acquittal in this case, we would have never lived it down, so naturally the senior prosecutors were rabid. Sam was walking around during this period like he was the man. He could do no wrong. And our guys—the good guys!—walked around with some serious egg on their faces. The media was all over this case, and rightly so. Headlines about the Bicycle Rapist had thrown the entire city into a panic, and after Gonzalez was caught, there was every expectation he would be put away for a long, long time. That justice had yet to be served, after the first three cases, only meant that everything was riding on the fourth case. Actually, Gonzalez had been charged in five attacks, but the fifth case was not a rape, it was sexual assault. What this meant, after having spent so much time in jail during the first trial, was that if the sexual assault charge was the only thing left on the table, he could have pled guilty and gotten time served. So a lot was riding on this fourth rape indictment. It was our last chance to put this scum away, and salvage a little bit of our reputations.

This was where I came in, and yet I wasn't handed the case to win it so much as to cover our butts in the likely event that we'd lose. There had been another prosecutor working the first trial, an attorney named Gail Ostriker. Gail was decent at her job, so there was no faulting her on her loss. There was, however, no good reason to send her out again, on what was essentially the same case, against the same defense attorney. To lose to Sam Gregory on the triple rape and then again on the last rape indictment would have made a bad situation exponentially worse—and left our office open to second-guessing, which is nearly as bad as losing in the first place.

My supervisor came to me one day and said, "We need a new thing on this bicycle rapist, Star. We're gonna throw it to you."

Me? I'd only tried one sex crimes case in my career

—the James Miller kidnapping in Brooklyn Heights, and that one was hardly a sex crime. It didn't make sense that they were throwing the Bicycle Rapist to me. "What's wrong with it?" I wanted to know.

"It's a dog," I was told. "You'll probably lose. It's our weakest case out of all of 'em."

The case was weak because we screwed it up—and because the victim was the quietest of the five. Mostly it was weak because of our negligence. The facts of the case were these: young woman; nineteen-year-old virgin; beautiful; Hispanic; five feet two inches; lived with her parents. Central Casting rape victim. This sweet young woman was driving her mother home in the family car. The defendant was on his bicycle. The mother got out of the car and went up to their Williamsburg apartment. It was a multiple-dwelling block, with apartment buildings all around, and several in this one complex. The victim, after dropping her mother off, went to park the car. The bad guy was on his bicycle, looking for his mark. He pretended to be hit by the victim's car, and fell to the street. The victim— bless her sweet, innocent heart—didn't realize the scam Gonzalez was trying to run and continued driving. But Gonzalez got back on his bike and followed the young woman all the way into her building. When she got on the elevator to go up to her apartment, he got in with her, and blocked her way with his bicycle. He then pulled a gun and forced her to the roof.

Meanwhile, the victim's parents started to worry. It wasn't like their daughter to be late, or to wander off. Only fifteen minutes or so had passed, but that was a long time to park the car and come upstairs. The mother had just left her. She was supposed to be right up. They went looking for her. A neighbor downstairs said they saw the girl come in. Her car was already parked. A sick feeling overcame the girl's father. Something told him his daughter was up on the roof, so he took the elevator to the roof to look for her. Sure enough, when he opened the heavy metal door to the roof, his worst fears were realized. Gonzalez turned and shot the father in the leg, and then he fled the scene.

Jump ahead to when Mr. Serial Rapist was finally caught. The victim and her father were both able to identify him. It appeared to be a strong case. We had the father coming up on the man raping his daughter, we had the father surviving the shooting, and we had the two corroborating testimonies. The only major problem was that whoever was handling the case from our office at the time didn't fully consider the fact that the father had cancer. Or maybe they did take it into consideration and figured they'd get a speedy trial and the father would still be okay, or that the girl's testimony would be enough alongside all these other cases. Even when it became clear that this poor man wasn't going to live to see the trial, no one thought to do a conditional examination. A conditional examination is when, in anticipation of an unavailable witness at the time of trial, prior to trial you take the testimony of the witness, allow the defense attorney to cross-examine, and file it all away, in the event that it's needed.

It was, it turned out, a scandalous error in judgment, because by the time we went to trial, the father was dead and William Gonzalez had been acquitted in the three other cases. Suddenly, we were looking at a case built around the testimony of a frail, frightened young girl. We couldn't use the father's ID, and the girl didn't even want to testify, and it looked to everyone in our office like a tanking case. Here again, the only way to win was to invest this poor girl with the kind of confidence and self-esteem she'd need to make a strong showing in court. I could have pulled out every trick in the book, but they wouldn't have worked. I could have argued the facts, but Sam Gregory would have deflected them. The defendant had walked on the first three cases, and Sam would have him walking on the fourth.

The key to the case, I thought, was to get the victim to want to put William Gonzalez away as much as the rest of us did, and the first move was to take her back to the scene of the crime. She hadn't been back since the night of the incident, and she hated like hell the thought of going through that heavy metal door and out onto that roof. She refused at first, but I was patient with her. I had my detectives with me, and I'd told them to take their time with things as well. The last thing I wanted was for this girl to pick up that one of the detectives didn't want to be there, or couldn't see the reason for her anxiety. She froze right there in the doorway. She was willing to try, but she just couldn't go through with it. Then she started to cry. I took her hand and I said to her, "The only thing that stands between William Gonzalez and a dozen other women is you walking through that door." So she sucked it up and walked through that door.

It was like a release. She cried, and in an instant the

demons of that horrible night were gone. We held each other. It really was a wonderful, empowering moment, and I had never been prouder of a witness. To this day, I thrill at what this poor, frightened young woman was able to achieve. Truly, she was scared to death to face this guy, but she battled back those fears to help see that other women wouldn't have to go through what she was going through. It was the key to the case, yes, but more than that, it was her key to putting it behind her.

Our next hurdle was the judge, Ann Feldman, who told me I'd only have two days to prepare for the trial. I'd just been given the case, and two days was outrageous. I needed at least a week, I said. I needed to spend time with my victim. I needed to assess the evidence, and mount a trial strategy. But the judge wasn't having any of it. "If you don't go to trial the day after tomorrow," she announced, that first day in her courtroom, "I'm letting Mr. Gonzalez out."

Sam Gregory, to his credit, had made an effective argument on behalf of his defendant. The man was indicted on all five cases at the same time, and he'd been in prison all these months, and now that he'd been acquitted of the first three cases, there was no reason to keep him in custody any longer than necessary. "I'll give you the time," the judge said to me, "but I'm still letting him out. If he walks, it's on you."

As long as she was leaving it up to me, then, I asked for two weeks. I mean, I didn't want to put this scum back on the street and risk his fleeing the jurisdiction, but at the same time I couldn't see giving the case anything less than my best shot—because then he would for sure walk. Sure, there was always the chance Gonzalez could flee to Puerto Rico, or somewhere out of the country, but I didn't necessarily take the judge's point that the defendant's possible desertion was my risk alone. It was her call as much as mine. I needed the time to adequately prepare, and she needed to do what she thought was right, which in this case was to let this guy out, seeing how he had already been acquitted of the three related cases. What neither of us counted on, though, was that Gonzalez was so cocksure that Sam Gregory would get him acquitted—as he had in the other three indictments—that he never missed a day in court. He was so convinced he could beat the charge and remain in New York, a free man, that he stayed put. To be sure, Sam was ethically bound to do what he could to keep his client in Brooklyn, but the reality is that the kid could have skipped town and there would have been nothing any of us could have done about it.

I used my two weeks to full advantage. I got inside my victim's head. We went over and over the details of that night, from every angle. We talked about what it meant to lose her father on the heels of her tragedy. We talked about how her family was coping, and where they would go from here. We talked about the lighting in the elevator, and the visibility up on that roof. We did everything we could to make sure there were no holes in her testimony, and no way this guy would walk a fourth time—that is, if he even bothered to show up.

Fortunately for us good guys, he did. He dragged his butt into court every single day. He was convinced he would beat this final thing, and be set loose on the streets of Brooklyn to get back to his sick business. I tried to look at him from my victim's perspective. Really, it must have been the hardest thing for her to have to pass him in the halls each day, to have to look him in the eye, knowing what he did and that he might get away with it. The very first day, it was like she was back on the steps leading up to the roof of her building, not wanting to go through that heavy metal door. She didn't want to do it, she didn't think she could do it, only this time she realized she had to do it. She was going to walk past him. And she did. She was wearing a black skirt, a white cotton blouse with a Peter Pan collar, a modest string of pearls, and little black pumps. We'd picked the outfit together, and I think it helped to fill her with a sense of confidence and purpose. She looked great, and ready to take on the world. She stepped out of that elevator and headed down the hall and looked the bad guy dead in the eye and walked right past him. She didn't flinch, and right at that moment I knew she'd be fine. However it went in that courtroom, she would be fine.

Sam Gregory's defense went pretty much the way he had played it in the other cases. It wasn't "he said/she said" in the sense that the defendant disagreed with the victim's account. "No, it didn't happen that way; it happened this way." Rather, it was "he said/she said" in the sense that we had the wrong guy.

I learned a long time ago that every case, no matter how complicated, came down to one or two things: what happened and who did it. Sometimes cases fell into both categories, but most of the time it was one or the other. This was a "who did it." According to the defense, Gonzalez was horrified at what had happened to my young victim. It was sad and tragic, but the defendant had no idea how it went down because he wasn't there at all. You could just hear the violins playing at the thought of Gonzalez losing one moment's sleep over what he had done to this young girl. It was the only argument Sam could make, and he made it well.

But we did our jobs pretty well too. In fact, my direct examination was probably the most successful direct examination of my entire career. It had to be strong, because everything was riding on it. It was all we had. I started to ask the victim about the incident. About interacting with the defendant out in the street. About getting in the elevator with this asshole. About going up to the roof. About how he forced her to perform oral sex on him, and then how he forced himself on her in the missionary position, face-to-face. My purpose was to show the jury that she had a lot of time to observe this excuse of a man—and every rea-son to pay careful attention.

There was one moment that seemed to bring the jurors around to the victim's side of the story. I asked her to describe the act, and she answered that she wasn't sure what I meant. We hadn't talked about this part of my trial strategy; I didn't think she could go through it twice, and I wanted her recollections to be fresh, real. "He had you down there on the concrete," I said, trying to help her along. "Tell me about your clothing. Tell me what that felt like."

Often, in a trial like this, the balance shifts on one tiny gesture, or one powerful phrase, and here we'd bumped into just such a moment. The victim described what she was wearing, and how the defendant had ripped off her underpants, and how uncomfortable it was to be forced down on the concrete in just that way. In her voice was the vulnerability she'd felt that night, the innocence she'd lost. She described how he'd kept his gun to her head the entire time, and how she looked up at him and tried to will herself up and out of her body. She kept trying to do this, she said, but she couldn't, so I asked her why.

"Because he was thrusting too hard," she said shyly.

"I don't understand," I said back, knowing full well what she meant.

She was at a loss for words, so she repeated herself. "He was thrusting so hard," she said again, only this time she started to move her head back and forth in a slight rocking motion, and her torso along with it, and every woman in the room knew exactly what she was describing. It was absolutely clear. She was a little girl, slight, and the defendant was a strong man, and she put an image in the heads of those jurors that they couldn't shake. Right then, one of the jurors crossed his arms in front of him and looked over coldly at the defendant, and in that moment I knew they would convict him. No matter what. This young girl was describing in graphic, physical terms having her innocence taken from her by this brutal act, and this was an essential point only she could have made to the jury.

Now, I don't want anyone reading this to think that for a rape victim to come across as believable on the stand she must also come across as virginal, because I don't believe that for one minute. No is no. It doesn't matter if you're a crackhead prostitute, if you say no to sex and the man forces you, it's still rape. It's just that in this particular case, with this particular victim, the trauma of her situation only added to her credibility. That she was a virgin at the time of the rape was one very important aspect of who she was and what had happened to her, and it vested her with the power to absolutely remember. My God, she remembered every last thing, in vivid, excruciating detail, and she went through it for me in such a powerful way that Sam Gregory couldn't touch her on cross-examination. He was a decent man, and he couldn't see hurting her any more than his defendant already had. About the only thing the defense could challenge was the victim's ability to identify her attacker. That was Sam's whole case, just as the victim's ability to remember was mine.

When it came time to sum up, the courtroom was packed. My colleagues from the DA's office filled one side of the room, while Sam's colleagues from Legal Aid filled the other. There were cops all around. Everyone even remotely connected to the case seemed to find their way into that courtroom to hear our closing statements, and as I looked back over my shoulder at the crowd I started to think it was like a title bout in Madison Square Garden. Sam had his people in his corner, I had my people in mine, and justice hung everywhere in the balance.

Sam offered a powerful summation. Really, he did an excellent, impressive job. His emphasis was that the victim did not have a good opportunity to observe her attacker, and was therefore unable to positively identify the defendant. No matter how close they were, he said, you couldn't trust her observations. There was only that short elevator ride, and that time on the darkened roof. That was the theme, and it was the right theme to take. It was the only theme to take.

I stood next, and I knew I had to do something dramatic. I walked to the juror's box and started speaking very quietly. There had been a lot of yelling and fireworks and I thought a quiet, reasoned tone would command just the right attention. I reminded the jurors of the testimony they'd heard on how long it took for the elevator to go from the lobby to the roof. The cops had timed it ten times, and it checked out at about fifty-nine seconds, so I got very close to one juror and took off my watch and set it down on the rail in front of him. "Mr. Gregory says fifty-nine seconds is not a long time," I very quietly said, indicating my watch. "So let's do a little experiment. I want you to imagine you're in the elevator with me. Don't look away. There's only the two of us in this elevator, and nothing else to see."

I paused for effect—because, honey, closing statements are always about effect—and waited for the second hand to reach the twelve. "The doors just closed," I said, my eyes locked on this one juror. I stared at him for a long time, and then I walked down in front and looked at the next juror. And the next. The courtroom was still and silent. All eyes were on my watch, and me. I walked to the next juror. After fifty-nine seconds, I finally said, "We're on the roof. Now tell me that's not a long time. Tell me you cannot describe every feature in my face."

This one I didn't get from any movie. This one I pulled out of the thin, tense air of the courtroom, out of desperation, but it had the desired effect. It didn't have to be scripted. It was real, and as I sat back down I had to stop myself from smiling, because I knew I'd nailed it. I was like one of those Olympic gymnasts after they stick a landing. Inside, I was bursting with smiles, but I had to keep cool on the outside until the results were in.

We stayed around that whole evening—me, the victim, the cops who worked on the case—waiting for the jury to come back. It took just a few hours, and I went back and forth between thinking this was a good sign and a bad sign. It was a clear ID case, without much room for deliberation. Either you saw it the victim's way or the defendant's. It could have gone either way, and in that long moment I imagined every outcome.

There is no moment in life quite like the stretch of time between when a jury returns and when the judge asks for a verdict. It is the longest, most agonizing moment, and when you're waiting with a vested interest for it to play out, it can be like suspended animation. The rest of the world is put on pause, and you're just hanging there. Even when you know you've nailed it, as I knew after my closing remarks, you start to think you never really know. You think you know. You say you know. But you never really know.

I looked over at the jurors, trying to get an indication of how it would go. Sometimes you get a tiny nod or a tight smile that gives the verdict away, but this time I didn't get anything. I knew but I didn't know. And I waited. Finally the foreman stood and read the verdict. Guilty of Rape One. Guilty of every single count on the indictment.

I turned to the victim and saw that she was crying. I reached out and held her hand, and then I turned to the judge. "Your Honor," I said, "we'd like the defendant remanded into custody pending sentencing." By now, I couldn't keep my smile down, because Judge Feldman had to put William Gonzalez's ass back in jail.

Then I motioned for the victim to come around the well of the court. I held her, and told her to look at the defendant. "Wave bye-bye," I whispered to her. "He's gone. You'll never have to worry about him again. He's done." And we stood there, waving good-bye to this scum, throwing it back in his face. It probably wasn't the most professional display, but I thought it would make this girl feel a little bit stronger after what had happened, and so I encouraged it.

She did me one better when it came time for the sentencing hearing. She found the words by which to measure her strength. She stood right in front of Gonzalez and stared him down and told him off big-time. "You tried to take my dignity, William Gonzalez," she said, "but you didn't. For so long now, you have been the subject of my dreams, and you've ruined them. Every night I go to sleep and I think of you and what you did to me. I think of what you took from me. Now, for a very long time, I will be the subject of your dreams, and you will have to think about this, because I will no longer dream about you." It was brilliant and powerful and real—and, gracious, I was so proud of her!

The judge was moved enough to sentence Gonzalez to sixty-six years in prison, which was the maximum. She wasn't supposed to take the three other cases into account in her sentencing, but she gave him every year she could give him, and I walked out of that courtroom hand in hand with the victim, feeling that together we could take on the world. Hell, she didn't even need me. Out of this brutal act, and in the course of the trial, she'd grown from a young girl to a vibrant, strong woman who had single-handedly saved dozens of women. I firmly believed that if this guy had been acquitted this time, he would have been right back on the streets and back to his brutality—and in all likelihood, in just a few months I would have been right back in that courtroom, seeking restitution.

My young victim might say that I taught her a lot during the trial, but she is the one who taught me. William Gonzalez didn't give this young woman her dignity, and he was powerless to take it away. More important, she reminded me that one person truly can make a difference, and this one person, this sweet young woman, truly did, and the message I took home with me that night was that you never know what you can do. This woman didn't think facing her attacker was something she could do, but she was wrong. What a phenomenal woman. She had it in her the entire time. Good for her, I thought. Good for all of us.

Pass It On

⚯

**Remember, no one can make you feel inferior
without your consent.**
—ELEANOR ROOSEVELT

THE BRAVE YOUNG woman who stood up against the Bicycle Rapist was not alone among rape victims in describing the phenomenon of going outside her body during her attack. I worked with many rape victims during my time in the district attorney's office, and victims of other violent crimes, and if there was any constant in their stories it was the burning need to remove themselves from what was happening, as it was happening. They got through it by thinking, This is not happening to me. This is happening to my body, but not to me.

In a certain way, that's what I try to do whenever someone tries to hurt me with his or her words or deeds. Obviously, the stakes are completely different, and I may never be in grave physical danger, but the method of coping is much the same. I get my back up and think, You can't change me by your actions. You can hurt me, but you can't touch me. My pride might be wounded. I might get irritated. I might even dwell on it for longer than I should. But there's so much good going on in my life, at the foundation, that it would take a helluva lot to shake me from my core. That was the lesson of that beautiful Hispanic girl up on that roof. What happened to her happened to her body but not to her soul; her soul was in such a good place before this animal abused her that nothing could take that away.

My first lessons on staying true to myself naturally came from my mother. People often ask me where I get my confidence, and I always point to Shirley. She filled me with such a tremendous sense of purpose and faith that there's no situation I can't face head-on. A violent attack on my body or a vicious attack on my character, it doesn't matter. I am vested with the notion that the world is mine. Nothing can change me. That came from my mother, and the way she put it in place was simple: She had her nose in my business, and an un-yielding pride in my accomplishments. I don't care what I was doing, Shirley was cheering me on. She pumped me up every day of my life; and she did the same for my sister, Sheila. She gave us the ammunition we needed so that if someone came after us later in life we would be able to go back to that place in our heart that she had made for us. We would be safe, and whole, and loved.

My sister helped define that place in my heart as well. Even though I had a few years on her, Sheila was always sticking up for me. She was a much stronger little kid, and I was a bit of a cornball. I liked books, museums, opera, the ballet . . . not exactly the formula for getting along as a little black girl in the housing projects—but exactly the stuff for getting your butt kicked, because everyone assumed you thought you were better than they were. I didn't think I was better, just different. I had different dreams. My childhood friends dreamed of three-bedroom houses in the suburbs; I dreamed of thirty-room villas in Versailles. My dreams weren't better, just bigger, and I was willing to do whatever was necessary to make them come true, and I had my little sister to back me up when my mouth got me in more trouble than my behind could handle.

Sheila's still backing me up. Her biggest fear is that somehow this TV pseudocelebrity ride I'm on now will hurt me, that some tabloid is going to cook up some story that will crush my spirit and make me doubt myself. I love her for it, but she needn't worry. As I have become an adult, I have found this untouchable place in my soul called "Starlet." I know her and I like her. I'm not the least bit concerned about someone who doesn't know me trying to define me. When you know who you are, no one can make you into someone you aren't.

And that's how it is. If a negative piece is written

about me in a newspaper or a magazine, or I hear a dismissive comment about my work, I go back to that center, that core, and I know those comments can't cut me. If I'm facing life-threatening surgery, I dwell on what I have to gain and not on what I have to lose. You can write what you want or say what you want or do what you want; you can even hit me with the longest odds in human history; I will still look at myself in the mirror and find something to feel good about.

Where did Shirley get the wisdom and the strength to pass such a precious gift to her daughters? The best I can figure is that it flowed from her parents, from her own childhood. See, the key to being a good parent is not money or education or creature comforts. It's being a good person. The first step in teaching your child to feel good about herself is to feel good about yourself. It's a simple equation. Your child's confidence will come from yours, and it won't matter where you live or what church you attend or what race you are.

My mother always managed to make her girls feel special. It's what she lived for. She used to dress me up, and mind you we didn't have the kind of money to dress me up in a fancy two-hundred-dollar party dress. No, dressing me up meant a pink ribbon in my hair and being told, "Look at that fabulous-looking girl!" That's what a little girl needs to hear, and I look around at the ways we live today and weep at how rare it is for little girls to hear that same message. I get on my little bandwagons from time to time, and the one that's bugging me right now is the way our advertising and fashion executives have managed to pluck the self-esteem from our children. They put out this arbitrary image of how young girls are supposed to look, and the young girls who can't quite manage it are left to feel inadequate, unworthy, second-rate. If Shirley were doing her "baseline" parenting now, she'd have her work cut out for her. Go to any newsstand, any month, and pick out a dozen magazines aimed at young women. What will you see? Articles on how to be thin, how to punch up your butt, how to make sure your thighs aren't chunky, how to get rid of flabby arms. This is what we are feeding our little girls.

I don't mean to generalize, but a lot of our top fashion designers are people whose preferences don't lean at all in my direction, or in the direction of many American women, yet they determine the tastes and lifestyles of our young women. I'm supposed to take fashion tips from these people? They drape their overpriced clothes on the bodies of tall, thin, flat-chested, no-ass-having girls and tell us this is what we're supposed to look like? Excuse me, but the message I take home is that these people don't care about me, because I don't look like that. I have an ass. I have breasts. My stomach is not flat. I look like a woman. And I've got news for these head-in-the-sand designers: Most women in America look a whole lot more like me than those flat-assed girls they're dressing with those clothes.

Even our subtle messages are off. We'll make a conscious effort to be politically correct, or socially correct, and say all the right things to our daughters about their weight and their healthy appetites, but they'll still hear us complimenting the women who fit the ideal. "Oh, you're so beautiful." "Oh, you're so thin. How did you lose that weight?'' ''Oh, my God, what do you do to keep it off?'' Well, yeah, but what we've just told the twelve-year-old girl who doesn't look like that is that she doesn't cut it. We won't ever tell her she's fat or she's ugly, because we're too careful for that, but we also won't tell her she's beautiful just the way she is. She won't hear you crowing about her the same way she hears you crowing about some girl you just saw in a movie, or on some billboard.

Let me give you some more evidence of Shirley's handiwork: If people didn't point out to me that I was full-figured, I'd never think about it. I read an article once that referred to me as one of the prettiest ''full-figured'' women on television, and I remember wondering what the hell the critic was thinking. I'm arrogant enough, or confident enough, or full enough of myself to think I'm one of the prettiest women on television. Period. End of sentence. Full-figured doesn't even enter into it, and that's because I was never made to feel as if my size determined my worth in any one area. As a matter of fact, as a little kid, I was a skinny thing. They used to call me Potail, because I had no butt. That was my Daddy Paul's name for me. I was his little Potail, and it wasn't until high school that I started to gain a little weight, but by that point it didn't really matter because I had Shirley's tremendous foundation on which to build. My dress size didn't matter to me because my dress size didn't matter to Shirley, and it didn't matter to my daddy either. Little girls get their first image of themselves as appealing to the opposite sex from the men in their lives. From their fathers. My dad got me to know from early on that I was "fine." I'm not talking cute or nice-looking; I'm talking fine! That's what my daddy says about my mother, that's what he says about my sister, and that's what he says about me. There is nothing that can make me smile like the feeling I get when the three of us dress up for a night out with Jimmy and he turns to us and says, "My women look *good!*" Baby, they don't make a pill that makes you feel that good about yourself. Even now, he watches me on the television and will call and compliment me on a new hairstyle or outfit. He'll say something silly like, "Girl, you were so sharp today, I almost cut myself watching you." Ridiculous, I know, but it makes my day.

Our little boys don't have to deal with these same messages, but they've got their own images to live up to. Athletic ability is probably the number one reputation-maker for boys in this country, and I suppose a dismissive comment such as "Oh, he's a wimp" can be just as damaging as "Oh, she's so fat."

So, for all you parents out there, take it from Shirley and Jimmy: Make it your business to know your child's business, and make sure they know how wonderful you think they are, how beautiful, bright, talented, athletic, smart, creative, loving, whatever. . . . Such constant confidence boosting is vital to the emotional health of our children, and I think back on it whenever I reassess my career as an attorney. Let's face it: Bad things happen to all kinds of people—kind, shy, uncertain. I had all kinds of victims sitting across from me in my office, in the middle of all kinds of bad situations, and the ones who handled those situations best were the ones with the rock-solid foundations and a firm sense of themselves. When I first met her, this young rape victim was terrified of confronting her attacker, but somehow she summoned the strength to overcome those fears and put the ordeal past her and move on. Something was passed down to her that gave her strength. It was in her all along, and it didn't take a crafty prosecutor to draw it out of her; it just took a little time.

. . . And Justice for All

c‍℘

Fairness is what justice really is.
—POTTER STEWART

It is easy to be popular. It is not easy to be just.
—ROSE BIRD

IN LAW SCHOOL, we all had to take a class on ethics, and I can remember going over the material with some of my classmates, and assessing the hypothetical situations they laid out for us, and wondering when we would ever face such dilemmas in a court of law. I grew up thinking the law was hard and fast, cut-and-dried, black-and-white, and even as I was being shown these gray areas I wasn't prepared to recognize them. It struck me as mostly ivory-tower, textbook stuff, and mostly irrelevant when put up against the kinds of issues we would be facing in the real world.

After law school, in addition to the bar exam, we rookies all had to pass something called the Professional Responsibility Exam, and here again the material was so far removed from what we would likely encounter in our day-to-day practice that it was hard to take seriously. Yes, it was interesting, compelling stuff, and I loved thinking my way through some of the complicated conundrums we were made to consider, but I couldn't shake thinking these types of problems would never come up. They all seemed so far-fetched, and the space between theory and practice was so great I could never quite see my way across.

At the Brooklyn district attorney's office, when I went in for my interview, I was actually given some of these hypotheticals to think my way through, and we were judged by our answers. I still thought to myself, Boy, nobody's gonna have to face this stuff on the job, but I wanted to show these people what I could do, the way I could troubleshoot these problems. These were some hard things, and yet if we didn't show the right kind of thinking in our responses we were out the door. Some of the questions were simple, as in, Do you move a piece of evidence when it's hurting your case? (Hint: Despite what we may or may not have learned from the O. J. Simpson case, the answer here is no.) And some of them were a bit more complex, as in, Do you disclose certain information that may or may not hurt your case? Well, sometimes it depends. There's a line, and it moves, and it's hard for young attorneys to understand that. Ultimately, I became a recruiter in the

DA's office, and I posed some of these ethical dilemmas myself, and I still thought they were rooted more in theory than in fact. I understood them for what they represented, even if I didn't see any practical application.

But do you know what? Not only does this stuff come up, it comes up all the time, and once you're out there, and working, it doesn't take long to find you. There are practical applications all around. There were two occasions, about midway through my legal career, one following soon after the other, that nicely illustrated some of the issues we had to face—and some of the ways different attorneys chose to face them. The first came in the middle of preparations for a murder trial. I was working the case with two detectives with whom I had worked before, and we had two thirty-something defendants in jail awaiting trial. These defendants were bad guys, from the neighborhood, and there was a sheet on each of them as long as my memory. I had a female witness putting both of these guys at the scene of the crime, but she seemed a little flaky—not untruthful, just flaky, but not so flaky as to discredit her testimony. We still had a pretty strong case.

As the trial approached, I interviewed a young man in my office who claimed to have information on the case. He was sent to see me by the attorney for one of the defendants, after the young man had gone to him with the same story. It happened, from time to time, that we were deceived by an unscrupulous defense attorney looking to throw doubt into our preparations, but I knew and trusted the lawyer involved in this case.

If he thought this was something I should look into, then this was something I should look into.

The young man appeared credible, and a tremendous source of information. He knew the players in the neighborhood, and he knew those streets, and he knew what happened. As a matter of fact, there's no way he could have known a lot of what he knew unless he was all the way plugged in, and the more I pushed him, the more I came to think we had indeed arrested the wrong men. The guys we had in custody were bad guys, no question, but I began to doubt their guilt in this one case. I even asked this late-into-the-game witness to submit to a lie-detector test and he agreed without hesitation. My favorite detective, Joe Ponzi, is the best polygraph guy in the business, as far as I'm concerned, so if he said you were telling the truth, that's all I needed. By the time the witness was through with the polygraph he had me and Ponzi convinced he was telling the truth.

My next step was a no-brainer. I moved to dismiss the case against the two defendants and reopen the investigation. I had no doubt these guys would have been convicted, the way I prepped my witnesses, but they didn't do the murder, so that was where the dilemma ended. It wasn't a matter of being able to prove it; it was a matter of doing the right thing, and I set this out not to pat myself on the back for taking the only just course available to me, but for the way people responded to my decision. For a week or so in there, I heard from all kinds of people—other prosecutors, defense attorneys, cops—many of them congratulating me on making a tough call, but where was the tough call in this? What choice did I have? These two guys weren't guilty, so they walked. That's just me doing my job. That's justice being served, and business as usual.

For some people, I suppose, the tough call lay not in dismissing the charges, but in investigating the young man's claims in the first place. We all had heavy workloads, and we all had a tendency to measure ourselves by the number of convictions we managed to bring back to the office. Under these terms, yeah, we had these two guys put away, so the dilemma might have been, Do you pursue it? Do you go down that road? Or do you leave things alone? So many of these last-minute witnesses are just blowing smoke anyway, so why even bother checking out what this one had to say? For some people the thinking might have been, Who really cares whether or not these guys did it? They were just two dumb "skells" from the neighborhood. If they didn't do this, they did something else; of this we were all certain. Oh, they were criminals; don't think they weren't. It's just that they weren't the particular criminals we were looking for on this particular crime. And let me be totally honest: These were black men. A disproportionate number of violent crimes in our inner cities are committed by black men. As a result, perhaps, there are a disproportionate number of bullshit arrests of black men, so if I had the opportunity to right a wrong for a black man, I was going to do it and do it proudly.

Still, it was astonishing to me that so many of my colleagues would have taken the case in a different direction, when really there was no choice to make. There was no choice at all.

A few weeks later, not incidentally, one of our mistaken suspects was involved in another murder, and this time we had him dead to rights, and the subsequent crime brought up all kinds of moral issues. The first murder—*my* murder—was still open, and here was this momentarily innocent guy who'd been caught in the system and faced a conviction and then put back on the streets, only to blow someone away for real. It's the kind of irony that makes you sick to your stomach, don't you think? And the question was put to me by my mother on the telephone the night I learned of the second murder. I spoke to Shirley every single day, as I still do, and she knew about the events surrounding the dismissal, and when she found out about this latest murder she asked me the question I'd already asked myself. "Do you feel guilty, baby?" she wondered.

No, in truth, I did not. I did the right thing—the only thing—and yet there was no getting around that if I had taken an easier course, a lazier course, this bastard would have been sitting on his behind in jail and this second victim would have been alive and kicking. The one move, the just move, led directly to a murder that could have been prevented, but was I the one vested with that preventing? No, I was not. Not even close. We don't live in a society where you can convict someone simply because they're a bad person. You convict them because they have committed a bad act, not because you think they're likely to commit a similar bad act sometime soon.

My next moral dilemma found me just a few months later. I was still working in Homicide, and about to try a robbery case that had gone bad and ended in a murder. We'd arrested four suspects in a robbery, during which a man was shot and killed. We were lucky. We had an eye witness who could identify three of the suspects. In addition, the fourth suspect ended up turning state's evidence on his buddies in exchange for leniency for himself. The three remaining guys were tried separately, and I pulled the third and weakest case of the three. The other two were convicted quickly because there was all kinds of evidence against them. But all we had on my guy was eyewitness testimony, and the testimony of his co-conspirator.

Still, we had a shot, and by the time I was handed the case the file was so unwieldy and disorganized, I had to spend my first day or so getting all the material in order. When so many DAs have their hands in a file, you never know what you'll find, so I was fairly systematic in my approach. One of the things we were always taught was to read reports again and again and again, on the thinking that each time you read it you'd discover something new. So I was always reading and rereading reports, and the more I read up on this case the more I became concerned. The identifying witness had given a clear ID of the other two suspects, but in those cases we also had a locker full of corroborating evidence. This third case was the one we absolutely needed him on because we had no other evidence beyond the accomplice testimony, and you can't convict someone based on accomplice testimony alone.

I called the witness into my office, as a matter of routine. He was a black man in his thirties. We sat around and started to get to know each other a little bit, and in the middle of our small talk I told him how impressed I was by his ability to recall all three of these guys. I was just making conversation, trying to make my witness feel comfortable, to feel good about himself, but as soon as I said it I wanted to suck those words right back into my face.

"Well," he said sheepishly, "I gotta tell you, this last one was hard for me. Probably couldn't have done it without the help of the DTs."

A bell went off in my head. I did not want to have heard what I just heard, and I did not want to put to this guy the question I knew I had to ask. By DTs, this man meant the detectives, and if they helped him in any way to make this identification, then we had no case. I knew we had the right guy—his buddies had all been quick to rat each other out—but without a proper ID we couldn't make a case against him. Remember, the accomplice testimony wasn't enough to convict, and the fact that his two partners had already been put away was irrelevant. If I asked the next question, I had to be prepared to hear the answer that would likely cost us the case. If I didn't ask, if I let the comment slide and pretended not to hear it or not to understand, then we still had something. But, of course, I couldn't let it slide.

I swear, I had all these thoughts bouncing around my head before I came out with the next question. It must have taken no more than a couple seconds, but it felt like minutes. Every possible scenario flashed through my head. My entire career flashed through my head. Law school. My Mama Muriel telling me that what a lawyer's supposed to do is get people out of trouble. My mother talking about how proud she was to see me take the oath to uphold the laws of the State of New York as an assistant district attorney. Everything flashed in just those few seconds, but I didn't miss a beat.

"What do you mean?" I asked. "The detectives helped you out?" There, it was out and in the room and up for discussion, and there was no turning back. A part of me felt the conversation might still go my way, but I had a sick feeling we were through.

"Miss Jones," my witness started in, "I don't think I'm supposed to be telling you this."

I thought, Well, I know where this is going. And then I reverted back to a style of speaking I sometimes used to put people at ease, especially black people. In my best Star the Home Girl voice I said, "Now, you know you'd better not let me get in that courtroom and look stupid in front of all these white people. How you gonna do a sister like that? I can handle it, brother, so tell me what happened."

Right away this man relaxed a little bit, because I'd defused the tension in what he had to say. It wasn't like it was the DA asking him to come clean. He wasn't gonna give it up to the Man, but this was just a sister. He'd give her the scoop. Star the Home Girl was playing it cool, but Star the DA was shaking, 'cause I knew what was coming.

"You know how you do the photo thing?" he said, describing the photo array he'd seen while picking out the suspects.

I nodded.

"Well," he continued, "when they showed me the photos, I couldn't identify anybody straight off, and the detective, he said, 'Look closely. Take your time with it.' And I looked again. I mean, I didn't get a good look at this guy. I seen him but I didn't get a good look at him, and the detective, what he did was he put his finger on the picture I was supposed to pick.'' The witness made a gesture to show how someone might push a piece of paper ever so slightly across a table to get you to pay specific attention to it, and I knew exactly what had happened. I'd watched enough cop shows to see how it could have happened. ''So that's the one I picked,'' he said. ''Anyway, I knew this was the guy they were looking at 'cause there was someone else who'd already picked him out.''

''How'd you know that?'' I wondered.

''The detectives told me,'' he admitted.

''So they showed you which guy to pick out?'' I asked, making sure. ''They told you he'd already been identified?'' He nodded, but that wasn't good enough. I needed him to say it. I tried again: ''Without the detectives, would you have been able to pick him out?''

''No,'' he said. ''I didn't see this one that well at all. The others I got a good look at, but not this one.''

He could see I was disappointed by his admission, even though I tried to hide it. I didn't think it was a good idea just then to let him know the magnitude of what he had just told me. I didn't want him to feel I was about to betray his confidence, or that our case was blown by what had happened, so I thanked him for his honesty and excused myself to go to the bathroom. It was a pretty lame excuse, but I needed to get out of my office and be by myself for a while, to think things through, only when I got to the bathroom there was nothing to think about. I knew what it meant. I knew exactly what it meant. And I knew this man was telling me the truth, even though I'd have to do the next checks. I just knew. So I sat down on one of the toilets and behind the closed stall door I started to cry. I cried like a baby. It wasn't like me to break down like that, but the tears just came, and when they stopped coming I stood and dried my face and went back to my office.

"You know what?" I said to my witness when I got back. "It doesn't look like we're gonna go to court in the next couple days, like we thought. It looks like we have some time on this." I was completely calm. To this day, I don't know how I was so calm, but I suppose the professional in me kicked in. I just wanted to get through it.

I didn't want to go to a supervisor until I checked things out with the detective who worked the case, so I called the man into my office. I closed the door behind him and got right to it. "It's come to my attention that you pointed out the photograph of the defendant to our witness," I said. I didn't ask if my information was accurate. I just put it out there, and his reaction gave him away. He dropped his eyes, then turned his head.

Now, this detective had retired in the months since he'd made the collar, and it was bad enough he'd messed up my case, but now he had me worrying that my doing the right thing and following this development to its conclusion would also mess up his pension. You know, this kinda thing just isn't done. It may be done on cop shows, but not in Brooklyn.

"I need to know," I said. "Did you do this?"

He swallowed hard, and then he spoke: "I would

never testify to this. I'd deny it if I was asked under oath, but your witness isn't lying.''

I sat back in my chair and looked at this man with a mixture of disgust and pain. I couldn't think what would possess someone to put our case on the line like that. And to hell with our case—I couldn't think what would possess someone to jeopardize his entire career.

He felt the need to explain. He told me he had made a promise to the woman whose husband was killed during the robbery. The woman was pregnant at the time, and the detective was understandably moved by her loss, and gave her his word he would get the people responsible. ''I told her I would get them all,'' he said, ''and I did. I got them all. Now it's up to you to keep it that way.'' He was a little arrogant about it, but I could see where he was coming from.

He left my office, and I cried again. Me, Star Jones, crying at work! And twice at that. I'm embarrassed to admit it, but at least I had the good sense to do it in the privacy of a toilet stall, and my own office. I never would have cried in front of those Homicide boys. Uh-uh. I don't think a professional woman needs to be tearing up every time something doesn't go her way. I find it manipulative when it's done to me, so I never do it to anyone else. Get a grip. You're a professional. Deal with things logically, not emotionally, and dry those damn tears. Which is exactly what I did. Next I went to my supervisors and told them what I had. I told the deputy chief what had occurred, that I'd asked the questions, that I'd gotten the answers. My supervisors all looked at me like they wouldn't want to be in my shoes for all the money in the world. ''We have no other evidence," I said, "but I'm gonna do everything in my power to find some other evidence."

In the meantime, though, I had to disclose this latest turn, and I had to disclose it the next time we appeared in court. I couldn't have this man in custody on the suspicion of murder without a valid ID. I had no doubt we had the right guy. None. And I had no doubt that with a clear ID we would have had a conviction. He didn't do the shooting, but he acted in concert. It was a felony murder. I hated to let this guy walk on a technicality, but technically speaking, that's what you have to do. What choice did I have? You always hear people say, "He got off on a technicality." Yeah, but that's what makes the law so great. You follow the law, Detective, because that's the backbone of our society.

And so I went into court the next day and I went over to the defense attorney and told him I was going to withdraw the identification. I didn't tell him why, and he didn't ask. He knew if I was pulling it there must have been a good reason. I didn't spell it out for him because I'd come to another decision, this one made in conjunction with my supervisors. We agreed that since this detective was already retired, and no longer in a position to hurt any other suspect or jeopardize any other case, there was no reason to ruin his pension. He was a good man caught in a promise he couldn't keep, in a case that just tore at his emotions. Other than this one misstep, he'd been a good cop, so we charged this one to his heart, not to his head.

Once again, if I hadn't asked the follow-up question, if the bell hadn't gone off in my head and switched me into detective mode, this case wouldn't have blown up on us the way it did. But I couldn't live with myself if I didn't ask those questions. I *had* to ask those questions, and I hate knowing there are a lot of lawyers out there who would have taken an easier path. How could anyone not ask those questions? The law is the law, and I'd rather let a guilty person walk than put him away illegally or unethically, because hidden somewhere in there is the chance that he might be innocent. We had this guy nailed, but we had him nailed mostly by an ill-gotten ID, so those nails had to come out.

The next day in court, I told the judge I was withdrawing the ID. I asked for more time to make my case. The judge knew something was up and gave me four weeks, but there was nothing else. I turned over every rock, chased every lead. I called back the detective who'd gotten the coerced ID, but he just confirmed what I already knew. "Don't you think I asked myself the same question?" he said. "If there was anything else, we wouldn't have needed his testimony."

But we did need that testimony, and now that it was gone I had to go and tell the family of the victim. Remember, this was the woman who was pregnant at the time her husband was murdered, and here I had to look in this woman's eyes and tell her I was gonna let one of the bastards responsible back on the street. I don't think I've ever been in as much pain as I was the day I had to tell that woman what had happened, but she surprised the hell out of me. She listened to what I had to say, and then she put her arms around me. She comforted me. She said, "I'm proud of you for doing what you're supposed to do." I was in pain for her and her family, but she said the pain was in losing her husband, not in losing this one bad guy to the letter of the law.

Man, you don't know what it's like to ride down in an elevator with someone you know participated in a murder, when you're the one who let his ass go. It was an agonizing moment, shot through with tension and second thoughts and reassessing. I couldn't let it go without saying something. I tried to catch this guy's eye, but when he met my gaze he looked away. He was ashamed. "You are one lucky bastard," I finally said. "You should make the most of it."

At this he looked up, and with what I took to be real sincerity he said, "I will." And then the doors opened and he stepped out, and I want to write that as I watched him disappear back into the world I knew he would turn his life around from this one moment, but the truth is I wanted to shoot him in the back. Really, that's what was running through my head at just that time: *If I only had a gun, I could shoot him in the back before he even makes it out of the building.*

I never heard from this guy again, but I like to think he did make the most of that free pass. In a way, it was a free pass for me as well. It allowed me to reaffirm my decision to become a lawyer in the first place. Everything I was, as a person and as a prosecutor . . . it all came down to this one case. That one moment, when I went ahead and asked that follow-up question, told me how much I'd grown on the job. It told me that all my talk about ethics and morals and integrity was built on something real. All those hypotheticals were built on something real. I think now of this defendant and I know he's out there, and I hope he did something with his life. He would have been locked up for a long, long time, and I hope he's a better person for the gift he was given. I know it made me a better person. It made me a better lawyer. It reminded me I was there on the job for a reason, and it had as much to do with the bad guys as it did with the good guys. The law is theirs as much as it is ours.

Don't misunderstand me: I don't always believe in rehabilitation, or second chances, or free passes. Sometimes—indeed, most times—the bad guys get what they deserve. I convicted some horrible, horrible people. James Miller? I'm glad that pervert is in the penitentiary for the rest of his life. John Ball? He belongs in prison. William Gonzalez? He deserves every one of his sixty-six years. But I am just as glad this one man was allowed to go free, because that's the reason I was there. I wanted to be the gatekeeper, remember? Well, those gates swing both ways, and sometimes you have to let someone out when what you've been taught is to keep him in. Because it's right. Because it's moral. Because it's just.

Pieces of the Same Pie

℘

We know what we are,
but we know not what we may be.
—WILLIAM SHAKESPEARE

PEOPLE ASK ME all the time how I see myself. Am I an African-American first? A woman? A Christian? A television personality? A lawyer? A southerner? A full-figured woman? Well, I'm all of these things put together, and then some—and the key to knowing who I am and what I stand for is the "then some." It's the combustible mix that we make of our lives that defines who we really are, don't you think?

In my case, most of these narrow descriptions make me bristle. I'm not *just* a television personality or *just* a woman. I have a relationship with God, but I'm not *just* a Christian. There's something dismissive in the way those words and phrases are tossed about—as if, somewhere deep down, they suggest more at what you are not than at what you are. I don't want to be thought of merely by my dress size, or the color of my skin, or the county of my birth, or the church I choose to attend. About the only definition I'm comfortable embracing is attorney. Give me a form to fill out, with room for only a one-word description of myself, and I'd write down "Lawyer." It's who I am, and what I've been, for as far back as I can remember, and it's how I see myself going forward, even though I haven't tried a case in years.

Obviously, the ways we see ourselves change as we pass through life. One day I might think of myself as a wife or mother. At one point, I was a daughter. I might have even seen myself as black, or female. On some days, above all else, I am a friend. On all days, I am His servant. These days, as I set these thoughts to paper, I'm a writer. Perspectives shift, including our own, but the abiding image I carry of myself is as a lawyer, and as I consider it now I wonder why. I guess it's the one thing about me that wasn't given to me. I got my race from my ancestors, my gender from Donald's sperm, my attitude from Shirley, my religious beliefs from those of my family, and my size from an underactive thyroid and too much bacon. But the law degree, that I earned. No one gave it to me, and no one can take it from me. It's not the same with this second career of mine, on television. Someone gave me this job, and if all you good people stop watching, or start writing letters to ABC telling them to get rid of me, they'll take it right back. So being a lawyer is what I'm proudest of, what means the most, what counts above all else; even if I never go back to it, there it will be. I relish my accomplishments as an attorney, and I will forever wear them on my sleeve. They're a part of me. They tell my story. These other aspects, they tell a part of the story, but they don't get to the heart of it.

You know, I hear from a lot of people who seem to want to cast me as a kind of spokesperson for big women in America, but that's not me. I suppose that would tell a part of my story as well, but to tell the truth, it's not a part I'm terribly interested in. My looks are important only for vanity's sake. Looks come and go. If I've thought about it at all, I've always thought about myself as an attractive person, and I do like to dress up and strut, but I've never focused on the size of my butt or the fullness of my hips or any of those particulars. I had a breast reduction, but only because my back hurt. (You try carrying around an award-winning chest since you were fifteen years old!) I choose not to focus on these kinds of things, because if I do, it allows other people to define me. But I define me. I look for that place within myself that makes me feel good, and I celebrate it and nurture it and let it take me to places I can only imagine.

For some people—perhaps even for you—that place might be your appearance. That's okay. If it matters to you, then it's essential to your sense of yourself, but if you've got killer eyebrows, and killer eyebrows are important to you, then you'd better make sure to maintain those eyebrows every week. If a washboard in your abdomen is a big deal, then you need to drag your gut to the gym every day. You have to find what's important to you, and you have to work to achieve and maintain it. No one else can give you that. My appearance is important—because, after all, a girl should be "fine," as my daddy likes to say—but my weight was never important to me. It wasn't even high enough on the list to be considered secondary. I have big hips, big boobs, and a waist that's too thick. The top designers don't even bother with the likes of me, so why should I care what a bunch of predominantly gay white men think about the way I look? Their opinion is just that, an opinion; that and a dollar-fifty will get me on the subway, if you know what I mean. If the consensus never tilts back in my direction, I'll still wake up in the morning feeling good about myself. If you define yourself, other people's opinions won't matter. You're no longer subject to fashion, or to the whims of taste.

I work out—because, like I've said, I'm no fool—but getting on the treadmill for me is not a matter of losing weight. It's a matter of health. It's helping to make my heart stronger, so I can walk up a flight of steps without getting winded. It's giving me the stamina to work all day on my feet. It's helping me to live longer so I can stick around and enjoy the fruits of my labor. I don't work out to fit myself into a smaller bathing suit, or to turn heads. I don't lack for dates. I'm happy with the men I attract, and they're happy with me. I may not have as many fashion choices available to me as some other women (although that will change when I design my own line of clothes), but I'm able to find clothes that accent my positives and give me the confidence I need to do the best job and create the best impression I possibly can.

I am happier in my thirties than I've ever been in my life, and do you want to know why? It's because I'm me now. At last. Everything I am, at this point, is within my own control. I control my reputation. I control my health. I decide what I want to do for a living, and where I want to live, and how I want to present myself. I choose how to spend my time, and my money. It's all on me. I'm the one who has to make the choices that will move me from one place in my life to the next, regardless of the circumstances of my birth. My parents can offer their support, but they can't make these choices for me anymore. My sister isn't around to help out when the neighborhood kids start making nasty comments. My sorority sisters can't back me up the way they did at American University. The little sixteen-year-old boy on the football team isn't here to validate my self-image as a young girl. All of this is now on me, and I love the responsibility of it.

Here, at last, I've found my center, and the trick, I've learned, is that I don't make anything in my life the entire pie. All the facets of my life are pieces of the pie, and if one slice of something has to go, there's still a whole hunk of pie to be enjoyed. It's when we make a single part of our lives the whole pie that we're left lonely or vulnerable when that aspect turns up missing. Relationships, friendships, career, family, religion . . . each part of my life has its place, and what's interesting in my personal pie is that the pieces don't have to be even, at any given time. Right now, for me, the professional slice is the biggest. Someday, the wife and mother slices will dominate. But I enjoy all the different tastes my life has to offer, and I enjoy them alone and in relationship to each other.

I was happy as a child, just as I am happy now, but as a child my happiness flowed from other people. My mother gave me a brand-new stereo. My father took me to a boxing match. Some boy asked me to the prom. Every time I felt good about myself it had to do with some nice thing someone else had done, but now it's on me. Now I have wonderful gifts of friends, and they make me happy, but I'm happy alongside them, not because of them. I am also happy when I'm alone. I did the final edit of this book all by myself at a café in Paris, with a bottle of champagne nearby. That for me, right now, is my idea of happiness. I have wonderful opportunities, but if I couldn't step up to the plate I wouldn't be doing what I'm doing, and I know that. I appreciate that. It's only with preparation that you can really and truly meet each opportunity head-on, and it's up to me to do the preparation. No one can help me with that anymore, and I find a tremendous satisfaction in this. A job well done is *my* job well done. No one can ever take that from me. They can take my job but they can't take the satisfaction that I did it well, that I made the most out of my opportunities that I possibly could. That's mine.

When people start arguing about affirmative action, I always say, "It gets you in the door, baby, but it don't keep you there." That's where preparation comes in, and I'm not a fan of quotas, for just that reason. Quotas keep you there. I'm a fan of affirmative action, because that gets you in the door; that's opportunity, but it's on each of us to meet those opportunities. All we need is a level playing field. Anybody who says we don't need a level playing field for blacks, Latinos, Asians . . . to give them opportunities to compete in arenas where they've never competed before, is delusional. No, you don't go setting aside ten seats over there for the Asians, and another dozen for the blacks, and maybe ten more for Hispanics. That's limiting, because there might be *two* dozen black people deserving those seats, so don't be telling me we only get twelve. To me, that's putting a ceiling on what any one group can achieve.

The right kind of affirmative action simply ensures that a special emphasis is placed on opening the doors of opportunity to all kinds of people. It's not a mandate as much as it is a consideration (Thank God I work for the kind of people who believe this—thank you, Barbara and Bill). If you're putting together a team of economists, and all you've got is a bunch of upper-class white people submitting names, then you're gonna wind up with a pretty same-seeming bunch of economists. Everyone will submit the names of the people they know, but they'll know people from the same background. They'll go to one kind of church, they'll get their hair cut by one kind of barber, they'll shop in one kind of grocery store. . . . Nine times out of ten, the names they'll submit will belong to people fitting within their own social setting. That's not necessarily a bad thing, that's just their experience, but affirmative action lets us expand the search a little bit, and open the doors somewhat wider, and consider whole other groups of people for our opportunities, and that's only a good thing.

I'll let you in on my special recipe, as far as my own pie is concerned. Inside every slice is the promise to make my momma proud every day. I don't see this as any kind of contradiction to wanting to define myself on my own terms, because a big part of that definition flows from my mother and the choices she's made in her own life. My self-image is a reflection of hers. It's mine, yes, but I can't ever lose where it came from; I see myself through my mother's eyes. Always have, always will. Whatever I do, whatever decisions I make, I want my mother to look at me and think, That's my baby. Nothing is more important. Shirley would be proud of me if I were busing tables, as long as I was the best damn buswoman I could be. My sister isn't a lawyer or a television commentator; she's a business-woman, and my mother couldn't be prouder. (Actually, Sheila has the edge nowadays, since she and my handsome brother-in-law Thomas gave my parents their first grandchild, my sweet nephew Terrell.) So you see, Shirley doesn't need me to be a well-known television personality or big-time lawyer, and I don't need to be these things for her.

I don't define myself by my station in life, because my mother never defined herself by hers. She taught me that the measure of a person is how they treat other people, and how they approach their jobs, and how they carry themselves from one station to the next. Hell, as a kid, I didn't know we were poor until I had the tools to recognize what money could buy. We had everything we could want. I thought we were rich.

Shirley loved me and my sister, and she encouraged us and gave us the sense of self to move mountains and overcome obstacles. Life doesn't get any richer than that.

I am an attorney at heart not because of what being an attorney has come to represent in our society. It has nothing to do with station or class or power, and everything to do with hard work and finding the right path and doing the right thing. I am who I am because of my dear, determined mother, and I aim to make her proud every day.

FOR ALL THE

little girls out there who are told they are

too dark, too light, too short, too tall,

too fat, too skinny, too smart, too dumb . . .

Tell them, not according to your Auntie Star.

Acknowledgments

There are a lot, so bear with me here . . .

First, Dan Paisner . . . for giving life to my words and thoughts; without you, this book would have still been an idea floating around in my head.

To Irwyn Applebaum, Barb Burg, Katie Hall, and the folks at Bantam Books . . . for your faith in me and my story. To Dan Strone . . . for selling the girl and the idea. To Jim Griffin . . . for guiding my career to places I've only dreamed about. To David Feinstein . . . for keeping the money straight. To Lisa Davis . . . for being the lawyer's lawyer.

To my assistants, Julie and Kristina . . . for keeping me organized. To my chief researcher Hank Norman . . . for keeping me up-to-date.

To James Blue . . . for discovering the television in me.

To Elizabeth Holtzman and Charles "Joe" Hynes, Michael Gartner, Don Brown and Jeff Zucker, Dirk

Zimmerman and Howard Schultz, Pat Fili-Krushel, Angela Shapiro, Valerie Schaer, and Holly Jacobs, and to Norman Brokaw . . . for touching my career at the right times in all the right places.

To Roger King for allowing me to sit at your knee and learn the business of television from the master. And to his wife Raemali for teaching me that a real Diva *commands* attention, not *demands* it.

To Barbara Walters for the opportunity to sit by your side and to Meredith, Joy, and now Lisa Ling . . . for being colleagues and friends. To Bill Geddie, Linda Finson, and the folks of *The View* . . . for the opportunity to do television that I'm proud of.

To the congregation at Cedar Grove A.M.E. Zion, Payne's Temple A.M.E. Zion, Shiloh Baptist Church, and Windsor Village United Methodist Church . . . for teaching me about God. To Kirbyjohn Caldwell . . . for helping me find God for myself.

To Dr. Ben Aaron . . . for saving my life.

To the women of Alpha Kappa Alpha Sorority, Inc. . . . for giving me the confidence to speak in front of a crowd, and clapping afterward.

To Susan Lucci . . . whose Erica Kane inspires me daily.

To Diahann Carroll and Oprah Winfrey . . . for opening the door and setting the standard.

To Karen Grigsby Bates, Evangeline Lilly, Deborah Norville, Denise Rich, and Blaine Trump . . . for being the wise women I go to for advice.

To Lela, Lita, Holly, and Cheryl . . . for backing me up, 24/7.

To Samuel L. Jackson and his wife LaTanya . . .

for being my big brother and sister, and taking those roles seriously.

To Leo . . . for the fun and friendship.

To Vanessa and Tony . . . for being my best friends and giving me the privilege of being yours.

To my nephew, Terrell, and my goddaughters, Ashley, Alexandra, Nia, Abi, Lauren, and Courtney . . . for being the future.

To my grandparents Clyde and Pauline and Paul and Muriel . . . for good genes.

To my sister, Sheila . . . for being the "wind beneath my wings" and never complaining about it.

To my daddy, Jimmy . . . for showing me what a man is supposed to be, and raising the bar so high that I'm willing to wait for the one who can reach it.

To my mother . . . for life and the example of how to live it.

Look for Reba's wonderful new book

REBA MCENTIRE'S

COMFORT FROM A COUNTRY QUILT

In this warm and friendly new book, Reba shares some of her most personal life experiences and shows how she faces many of today's challenges by drawing wisdom and strength from the precious values and traditions of her country past.

This is a certain keepsake book of wisdom, entertainment, and inspiration for every Reba fan.

Available now wherever Bantam books are sold

Printed in the United States
by Baker & Taylor Publisher Services